وَمَا أَرْسَلْنَاكَ إِلَّا رَحْمَةً لِلعَالَمِينَ

"We sent You not but as a mercy to all the Worlds"

قِصَّةُ

مَولِدِ النَّبِيِ ﷺ

للشَيخ الوَلي المُحَدِّث عبد الرَّحمَن الدَّيْبَعِي

Mawlid ad-Daybaʿī

Story of the Birth of Prophet Muḥammad ﷺ and a Description of His Excellent Qualities

Shaykh ʿAbd ar-Raḥmān ad-Daybaʿī

Compiled by
Shaykh Muhammad Hisham Kabbani

With Original Songs by
Ali al-Sayed

INSTITUTE FOR SPIRITUAL AND CULTURAL ADVANCEMENT

ISBN: 1-930409-43-5

ISCA
Institute for Spiritual and Cultural Advancement

Published and Distributed by:
Institute for Spiritual and Cultural Advancement
17195 Silver Pkwy, #401
Fenton, MI 48430
(810) 593-1222

Shaykh Muhammad Nazim Adil al-Haqqani with his son-in-law, Shaykh Muhammad Hisham Kabbani (right), and his brother, Shaykh Muhammad Adnan Kabbani (left).

Contents

Transliteration

To simplify reading the Arabic names, places and terms are not transliterated in the main text. Transliteration is provided in the section on the spiritual practices to facilitate correct pronunciation and is based on the following system:

Symbol	Transliteration	Symbol	Transliteration	Vowels:	
				Long	
ء	'	ط	ṭ	آ ى	ā
ب	b	ظ	ẓ	و	ū
ت	t	ع	ʿ	ي	ī
ث	th	غ	gh	Short	
ج	j	ف	f	َ	a
ح	ḥ	ق	q	ُ	u
خ	kh	ك	k	ِ	i
د	d	ل	l		
ذ	dh	م	m		
ر	r	ن	n		
ز	z	ه	h		
س	s	و	w		
ش	sh	ي	y		
ص	ṣ	ة	ah; at		
ض	ḍ	ال	al-/'l-		

Introduction

The cousin of Sayyidina Muḥammad ﷺ, Al-ʿAbbās ibn ʿAbd al-Muṭṭalib ؓ said:

And then, when you were born,
a light rose over the earth
until it illuminated the horizon
with its radiance.
We are in that illumination
and that original light
and those paths of guidance
and thanks to them
we pierce through.

The poet of the Prophet ﷺ Ḥassan ibn Thābit ؓ said:

(I swear) By Allāh, no woman
has conceived and given birth
To one like the Messenger,
the Prophet and guide of his people.
Nor has Allāh created
among his creatures
One more faithful
to his sojourner
or his promise
Than he who was
the source of our light.

In this blessed tradition of our ancestors and the predecessors in the faith, we present this book of magnificent poetry and verse dedicated to the love of our Master, and Master of All Creation, Prophet Muḥammad, upon whom be the choices of Allāh's peace and blessings, and upon his family, companions, House and followers, up to the Day of Rising.

I humbly dedicate this work to my beloved Master, Shaykh of the Age and Protector of the Prophetic Path, Cleaver to the Tradition and the Group, Savior of the Age, and Keeper of the Secrets of Divine Immanence and Prophetic Providence, Mawlana Sulṭān al-Awlīyā, Shaykh Muḥammad Nāẓim ʿAdil al-Ḥaqqānī, with all my love and devotion.

Shaykh Muḥammad Hisham Kabbani
Chairman, Institute for Spiritual and Cultural Advancement (ISCA)
Beirut, Lebanon
Jumada al-Awwal 15, 1425/June 22, 2006

1 - The Opening

بسمِ اللهِ الْرَّحْمَنِ الرَّحِيْمِ

Bismillāhi ′r-Raḥmāni ′r-Raḥīm

(1) الْفَاتِحَةُ لَنَا وَلَكُمْ يَا حَاضِرِين

(1) Al-Fātiḥatu lanā wa lakum yā ḥāḍirīn
[Recite] the Opening [chapter of Qur'an] for our benefit and for yours, O attendees together,

(2) وَلِوَالِدِينَا وَوَالِدِيكُمْ، وَلأَهَالِينَا وَلأَولادِنَا

(2) wa li-wālidīnā wa-wālidīkum, wa li-ahālīnā wa li-awlādinā
And for our parents and your parents and for our families and for our children,

(3) وَلِمَشَايِخِنَا وَلِمَنْ حَضَرَنَا وَلِمَنْ غَابَ عَنَّا

(3) wa li-mashāyikhinā wa limān ḥaḍaranā wa liman ghāba ʿanna
And for our shaykhs and for whoever is attending [this gathering] with us and for whoever is absent,

(4) وَلأَحيائِنَا وَلأَمْواتِنَا وَلِلمُوَاظِبِينَ عَلَى هَذَا المَجلِسْ وَلِمَنْ كَانَ سَبَبًا فِيْ جَمعِنَا

(4) wa li-aḥyā′inā wa li-amwātinā wa li ′l-muwāẓibīna ʿalā hādhā ′l-majlis wa liman kāna sababan fī jamʿinā
And for our living ones and our deceased ones and for those who are consistant in attending this gathering and for whoever was a cause for our coming together

(5) بِأَنَّ اللهَ الْكَرِيمَ يُنَوِّرُ القُلُوبَ، وَيَغفِرُ الذُّنُوبَ، وَيَحفَظُنَا بِمَا حَفِظَ بِهِ الذِّكر وَيَنصُرُنَا بِمَا نَصَرَ بِهِ الرُّسُلَ

(5) bi-anna Allāhal-karīma yunawwiru ′l-qulūb, wa yaghfiru ′dh-dhunūb, wa yasturu′l-ʿuyyūb wa yaḥfaẓunā bimā ḥafiẓa bihi ′dh-dhikr wa yanṣurunā bimā naṣar bihi ′r-rusul
And that Allāh the Most Generous enlighten the hearts and forgive the sins and that He protect us in the same manner he safeguarded the Quran, and that He supports and gives us victory in the same manner He supported and gave victory to His prophets,

(6) وَأَنَّ اللهَ الكَرِيمَ يَجعَلُ مَجلِسَنَا هَذَا مُحَاطًا بِالخَيرَاتِ وَالمَسَرَّاتِ وَالأَنْوَارِ وَالبَرَكَاتِ، وَيَقضِيْ لَنَا جَمِيعَ الحَاجَاتِ، بِجَاهِ خَيرِ البَرِيَّاتِ

(6) wa-anna Allāha 'l-karīma yaj'alu majlisanā hādhā muḥātan bi 'l-khayrāti wa 'l-masarrat wa 'l-anwāri wa 'l-barakāt wa yaqḍi lanā jamī'a 'l-ḥājāt bi-jāhi khayri 'l-bariyyāt

And that Allāh the most Generous cause this gathering to be encompassed by goodnesses and happinesses and lights and blessings and that He takes care of all our needs for the sake of the Best one of all creation

(7) وَأَنَّ اللهَ يَنصُرُ المُسلِمِينَ

(7) wa-anna Allāha yanṣuru 'l-muslimīn

And that Allāh will support and give victory to those who submit [to Him]

(8) وَعَلَى نِيَّةِ أَنَّ اللهَ الْكَرِيمَ يَنْصُرُ سُلطَانَ الأَوْلِيَاء الشَّيخْ مُحَمَّدْ نَاظِمْ عَادِلَ الحَقَّانِي، وَيَحفَظُهُ وَيُوَفِّقُهُ عَلَى الدَّوَامِ بِجَاهِ خَيرِ الأَنَامِ

(8) wa 'alā niyyati anna Allāha 'l-karīma yanṣuru sulṭāna al-awliyā' ash-Shaykh Muḥammad Nāẓim 'Ādil al-Ḥaqqānī, wa yaḥfaẓuhu wa yuwaffiquhu 'alā 'd-dawām bi-jāhi khayri 'l-anām,

And with the intention that Allāh the Most Generous support our master the Sultan of Saints, Shaykh Muḥammad Nāẓim 'Adil al-Ḥaqqānī and protect and preserve him and make him successful for all time for the sake of the Best of all created beings,

(9) وَعَلَى كُلِّ نِيَّةٍ صَالِحَةٍ مَعْ حُسنِ الخَاتِمَةِ عِندَ المَوتِ بَعدَ العُمرِ المَدِيدِ فِيْ طَاعَةِ اللهِ، وَإِلَى حَضْرَةِ النَبِيِّ. الفَاتِحَةْ!

(9) wa 'alā kulli niyyatin ṣāliḥatin m'a ḥusni 'l-khātimat 'inda 'l-mawt b'ada 'l-'umri 'l-madīd fī ṭā'atillāh wa ila ḥaḍrati 'n-nabīyyi 'l-Fātiḥa.

(9) and on every pure intention with most perfect of endings at the time of passing from this life after a long life in service and obedience to God, and to the ever-present Prophet, [recite] al-Fātiḥa.

2 - The Opening Qaṣīda

قَصِيدَةُ الإِفْتِتَاحْ

(1) يَا رَبِّ صَلِّ عَلَى مُحَمَّد

(1) Yā Rabbi ṣalli ʿalā Muḥammad

O Lord, bestow blessings upon Muḥammad.

(2) يَا رَبِّ صَلِّ عَلَيْهِ وَسَلِّمْ

(2) Yā Rabbi ṣalli ʿalayhi wa sallim

O Lord, bestow blessings and peace be upon him.

(3) يَا رَبِّ صَلِّ عَلَى مُحَمَّد يَا رَبِّ بَلِّغْهُ الْوَسِيْلَة

(3) Yā Rabbi ṣalli ʿalā Muḥammad Yā Rabbī balligh-hu ʾl-wasīlah

O Lord, bestow blessings upon Muḥammad.
O Lord, grant him alone the station of interceding.[1]

(4) يَا رَبِّ صَلِّ عَلَى مُحَمَّد يَا رَبِّ خُصَّهُ بِالْفَضِيْلَة

(4) Yā Rabbi ṣalli ʿalā Muḥammad Yā Rabbī khuṣṣah bi ʾl-faḍīlah

O Lord, bestow blessings upon Muḥammad.
O Lord, favor him abovre all the creations.[2]

(5) يَا رَبِّ صَلِّ عَلَى مُحَمَّد يَا رَبِّ وَارْضَ عَنِ الْصَّحَابَة

(5) Yā Rabbi ṣalli ʿalā Muḥammad Yā Rabbī wa ʾarḍā ʿani ʾṣ-ṣaḥābah

O Lord, bestow blessings upon Muḥammad.
O Lord, may You be pleased with the companions.

(6) يَا رَبِّ صَلِّ عَلَى مُحَمَّد يَا رَبِّ وَارْضَ عَنِ الْسُّلالَة

(6) Yā Rabbi ṣalli ʿalā Muḥammad Yā Rabbī wa ʾarḍā ʿani ʾs-sulālah

O Lord, bestow blessings upon Muḥammad.
O Lord, may You be pleased with his descendents.

(7) يَا رَبِّ صَلِّ عَلَى مُحَمَّد يَا رَبِّ وَارْضَ عَنِ الْمَشَايِخ

[1] *Al-Wasīlah - a* rank that Allah has promised in the Hereafter or the Heavens for Sayyidina Muḥammad ﷺ by which he will intercede on behalf of the sinners of the Ummah.

[2] *Al-Faḍīlah* - an outstanding eminent position that goes with the Station of *Wasīlah*.

(7) Yā Rabbi ṣalli ʿalā Muḥammad   Yā Rabbī wa ʾarḍā ʿani ʾl-mashāyikh

O Lord, bestow blessings upon Muḥammad.
O Lord, may You be pleased with the masters.

(8) يَا رَبِّ صَلِّ عَلى مُحَمَّد   يَا رَبِّ فَارْحَمْ وَالِدِينَا

(8) Yā Rabbi ṣalli ʿalā Muḥammad   Yā Rabbi farḥam wālidīna

O Lord, bestow blessings upon Muḥammad.
O Lord, may You have mercy on our parents.

(9) يَا رَبِّ صَلِّ عَلى مُحَمَّد   يَا رَبِّ وَارْحَمْنَا جَمِيعاً

(9) Yā Rabbi ṣalli ʿalā Muḥammad   Yā Rabbi warḥamnā jamīʿan

O Lord, bestow blessings upon Muḥammad.
O Lord, may You have mercy on all of us.

(10) يَا رَبِّ صَلِّ عَلى مُحَمَّد   يَا رَبِّ وَارْحَمْ كُلَّ مُسْلِم

(10) Yā Rabbi ṣalli ʿalā Muḥammad   Yā Rabbi warḥam kulla Muslim

O Lord, bestow blessings upon Muḥammad.
10. O Lord, may You have mercy on all Muslims,

(11) يَا رَبِّ صَلِّ عَلى مُحَمَّد   يَا رَبِّ وَاغْفِرْ لِكُلِّ مُذْنِب

(11) Yā Rabbi ṣalli ʿalā Muḥammad Yā Rabbi waghfir li-kulli mudhnib

O Lord, bestow blessings upon Muḥammad.
O Lord, and forgive every sinner.

(12) يَا رَبِّ صَلِّ عَلى مُحَمَّد   يَا رَبِّ يَا سَامِعْ دُعَانَا

(12) Yā Rabbī ṣalli ʿalā Muḥammad   Yā Rabbi yā sāmiʿ duʿānā

O Lord, bestow blessings upon Muḥammad.
O Lord, O Hearer of our supplication!

(13) يَا رَبِّ صَلِّ عَلى مُحَمَّد   يَا رَبِّ لا تَقْطَعْ رَجَانَا

(13) Yā Rabbi ṣalli ʿalā Muḥammad   Yā Rabbi lā taqṭaʿ rajānā

O Lord, bestow blessings upon Muḥammad.
O Lord, may You not end our hopes.

(14) يَا رَبِّ صَلِّ عَلى مُحَمَّد   يَا رَبِّ بَلِّغْنَا نَزُورُه

(14) Yā Rabbi ṣalli ʿalā Muḥammad   Yā Rabbi ballighnā nazūruh

O Lord, bestow blessings upon Muḥammad.
O Lord, may You send us to visit him at his resting place.

(15) يَا رَبِّ صَلِّ عَلى مُحَمَّد   يَا رَبِّ تَغْشَانَا بِنُوْرِه

(15) Yā Rabbi ṣalli ʿalā Muḥammad Yā Rabbi taghshānā bi nūrih
O Lord, bestow blessings upon Muḥammad.
O Lord may You dress us with his light.

(16) يَا رَبِّ صَلِّ عَلى مُحَمَّد   يَا رَبِّ حِفْظَانَكْ وَامَانَكَ

(16) Yā Rabbi ṣalli ʿalā Muḥammad Yā Rabbi ḥifẓānak wa amānak
O Lord, bestow blessings upon Muḥammad.
O Lord, may You safeguard us with Your security (peace).

(17) يَا رَبِّ صَلِّ عَلى مُحَمَّد   يَا رَبِّ وَاسْكِنَّا جِنَانِك

(17) Yā Rabbi ṣalli ʿalā Muḥammad Yā Rabbi wa 'skinnā jinānak
O Lord, bestow blessings upon Muḥammad.
O Lord, may You let us reside in your heavens.

(18) يَا رَبِّ صَلِّ عَلى مُحَمَّد   يَا رَبِّ أجِرْنَا مِنْ عَذَابِك

(18) Yā Rabbi ṣalli ʿalā Muḥammad Yā Rabbi 'ajirnā min ʿadhābik
O Lord, bestow blessings upon Muḥammad.
O Lord, may You exclude us from Your punishment.

(19) يَا رَبِّ صَلِّ عَلى مُحَمَّد   يَا رَبِّ وَارْزُقْنَا الْشَّهَادَة

(19) Yā Rabbi ṣalli ʿalā Muḥammad Yā Rabbi warzuqnā 'ash-shahādah
O Lord, bestow blessings upon Muḥammad.
O Lord, may You grant us with the station of the martyrs.

(20) يَا رَبِّ صَلِّ عَلى مُحَمَّد   يَا رَبِّ حِطنَا بِالسَّعَادَة

(20) Yā Rabbi ṣalli ʿalā Muḥammad Yā Rabbi ḥiṭnā bis-saʿādah
O Lord, bestow blessings upon Muḥammad.
O Lord, may You envelop us with happiness.

(21) يَا رَبِّ صَلِّ عَلى مُحَمَّد   يَا رَبِّ وَاصْلِحْ كُلَّ مُصْلِح

(21) Yā Rabbi ṣalli ʿalā Muḥammad Yā Rabbi waṣliḥ kulla muṣliḥ
O Lord, bestow blessings upon Muḥammad.
O Lord, may You reform those who wish to change (themselves).

(22) يَا رَبِّ صَلِّ عَلى مُحَمَّد   يَا رَبِّ وَاكْفِ كُلَّ مُؤذِ

(22) Yā Rabbi ṣalli ʿalā Muḥammad Yā Rabbi wakfī kulla mū'dhī
O Lord, bestow blessings upon Muḥammad.
O Lord, may You protect us from every harmful one.

(23) يَا رَبِّ صَلِّ عَلى مُحَمَّد   يَا رَبِّ نَخْتِمْ بِالْمُشَفَّع

(23) Yā Rabbi ṣalli ʿalā Muḥammad   Yā Rabbi nakhtim bi 'l-mushaffa'

O Lord, bestow blessings upon Muḥammad.
O Lord, we end with the name of the Prophet who intercedes.

(24) يَا رَبِّ صَلِّ عَلى مُحَمَّد   يَا رَبِّ صَلِّ عَلَيْهِ وَسَلِّم

(24) Yā Rabbi ṣalli ʿalā Muḥammad   Yā Rabbi ṣalli ʿalayhi wa sallim

O Lord, bestow blessings upon Muḥammad.
O Lord, bestow blessings upon him and grant him peace.

اللهُمَّ صَلِّ وَسَلِّمْ وَبَارِكْ عَلَيْهِ وَعلَىْ آلِه

Allāhuma ṣalli wa sallim wa bārik ʿalayhi wa ʿalā ālih

O Allāh raise higher, bless and send peace on him and his family

3 - Allāh Praises His Prophet

أَعُوذُ بِاللهِ مِنَ الشَّيْطَانِ الرَّجِيمِ

بِسْمِ اللهِ الرَّحْمٰنِ الرَّحِيمِ

āʿūdhu billāhi mina'sh-shayṭāni 'r-rajīm
Bismillāhi 'r-Raḥmāni 'r-Raḥīm
I seek the protection of Allāh from the accursed Satan
In the name of God, the Beneficent, the Merciful

(1) إِنَّا فَتَحْنَا لَكَ فَتْحاً مُّبِيناً

(1) Innā fataḥnā laka fatḥan mubīnā
Verily We have granted Thee a manifest victory. (48:1)

(2) لِيَغْفِرَ لَكَ اللَّهُ مَا تَقَدَّمَ مِن ذَنبِكَ وَمَا تَأَخَّرَ وَيُتِمَّ نِعْمَتَهُ عَلَيْكَ وَيَهْدِيَكَ صِرَاطاً مُّسْتَقِيماً

(2) li-yaghfira laka 'l-Lāhu mā taqaddama min dhanbika wa mā ta'akhkhara wa yutimma niʿmatahu ʿalayka wa yahdīyaka ṣirāṭan mustaqīma
So that Allāh may grant you forgiveness for your faults of the past and for those in the future; and to perfect His favour upon you; and to guide onto a Straight path; (48:2)

(3) وَيَنصُرَكَ اللَّهُ نَصْراً عَزِيزاً

(3) wa yanṣuraka 'l-Lāhu naṣran ʿazīza
And Allāh will support you with a mighty victory. (48:3)

(4) لَقَدْ جَاءكُمْ رَسُولٌ مِّنْ أَنفُسِكُمْ عَزِيزٌ عَلَيْهِ مَا عَنِتُّمْ حَرِيصٌ عَلَيْكُم بِالْمُؤْمِنِينَ رَؤُوفٌ رَّحِيمٌ

(4) laqad jā'akum rasūlun min anfusikum ʿazīzun ʿalayhi mā ʿanittum ḥarīṣun ʿalaykum bi 'l-mu'minīna Ra'ūfun Raḥīm
A Messenger from yourselves has come to you: it grieves him that you should perish: ardently anxious is he over you: to the Believers is he most kind and merciful. (9:128)

(5) فَإِن تَوَلَّوْاْ فَقُلْ حَسْبِيَ اللّهُ لا إِلَـهَ إِلاَّ هُوَ عَلَيْهِ تَوَكَّلْتُ وَهُوَ رَبُّ الْعَرْشِ الْعَظِيمِ

(5) Fa 'in tawallaw fa-qul ḥasbiya 'l-Lāhu lā ilāha 'illa Huwa 'alayhi tawakkaltu wa Huwa Rabbu 'l-'Arshi'l-'Aẓīm

But if those [who are bent on denying the truth] turn away, say: "God is enough for me! There is no deity save Him. In Him have I placed my trust, for He is the Sustainer, in awesome almightiness enthroned." (9:129)

(6) إِنَّ اللَّهَ وَمَلَائِكَتَهُ يُصَلُّونَ عَلَى النَّبِيِّ يَا أَيُّهَا الَّذِينَ آمَنُوا صَلُّوا عَلَيْهِ وَسَلِّمُوا تَسْلِيما.

(6) 'Inna 'l-Lāha wa malā'ikatahu yuṣallūna 'alān-Nabiy yā ayyuha 'l-ladhīna 'āmanū ṣallū 'alayhi wa sallimū taslīmā.

Allāh and His angels send blessings on the Prophet: O ye that believe! Send ye blessings on him, and salute him with all respect. (33:56)

اللهُمَّ صَلِّ وَسَلِّمْ وَبَارِكْ عَلَيْهِ وَعلَىْ آلِه

Allāhuma ṣalli wa sallim wa bārik 'alayhi wa 'alā ālih

O Allāh raise higher, bless and send peace on him and his family

4 - His Creation

اللهُمَّ صَلِّ وَسَلِّمْ وَبَارِكْ عَلَيْهِ وَعلَىْ آلِه

Allāhuma ṣalli wa sallim wa bārik ʿalayhi wa ʿalā ālih

O Allāh raise higher, bless and send peace on him and his family

(1) الْحَمْدُ للهِ القَوِيِّ الْغَالِبْ

(1) Al-ḥamdu lillāhi ʾl-Qawīyyi ʾl-Ghālib

All praise belong to Allāh, Who is Strong and Dominant,

(2) الْوَلِيِّ الْطَالِبْ

(2) Al-Waliyyi ʾT-ṭālib

He The Protecting Friend, The Sought after One.

(3) الْبَاعِثِ الوَارِثِ المَانِحِ السَّالِبْ

(3) Al-Bāʿithi ʾl-Wārithi ʾl-Mānihi ʾs-sālib

He is the Resurrector, The Inheritor, the Giver (of blessings) and Remover of our bereavement,

(4) عَالِمِ الكَائِنِ وَالبَائِنِ وَالْزَّائِلِ وَالذَّاهِبْ

(4) ʿĀlimi ʾl-kāʾini wa ʾl-bāʾini waz-zāʾili wa ʾdh-dhāhib

He is the Knower of all beings be they in the current, transient or passed events.

(5) يُسَبِّحُهُ الآفِلُ وَالمَائِلُ وَالطَّالِعُ وَالْغَارِبْ

(5) yusabbiḥuhu ʾl-ʾāfilu wa ʾl-māʾilu wa ʾṭ-ṭāliʿu wa ʾl-ghārib

All the stars invoke His praises, those on the incline, those ascending and those setting.

(6) وَيُوَحِّدُه النَّاطِقُ وَالصَّامِتُ وَالجَامِدُ والْذَّائِبْ

(6) wa yuwaḥḥiduhu ʾn-nāṭiqu wa ʾṣ-ṣāmitu wa ʾl-jāmidu wa ʾdh-dhāʾib

All possessed of speech profess His Oneness, as do the silent, the solid and the liquid

(7) يَضْرِبُ بِعَدْلِهِ السَّاكِنَ وَيَسكُنُ بِفَضْلِهِ الضَّارِبْ

(7) yaḍribu bi-ʿadlihi 's-sākinu wa yaskunu bi-faḍlihi 'ḍ-ḍārib;
By His Justness He moved the stationary and with His Bounty causes the moving to come to rest.

(8) * (لاَ إلهَ إلاَّ الله) * حَكِيمٌ أظْهَرَ بَدِيعَ حِكَمِهِ وَالعَجائِبْ

(8) <u>Lā ilāha illa 'l-Lāh</u>; Hakīmun aẓhara badīʿa ḥikamihi wa 'l-ʿajā'ib
(There is no god but Allāh) [the] Wise One Whose Wisdom manifest in the wonders of His creations and wonder.

(9) فِي تَرْتِيبِ تَرْكِيبِ هَذِهِ الْقَوَالِبْ

(9) fī tarkībi tartībi hādhihi 'l-qawālib
In the orderly arrangement and assembly of His creations:

(10) خَلَقَ مُخًّا وَعظْماً وَعَضُداً وَعُرُوقاً وَلَحْمًا وَجِلْدًا وَشَعْرًا وَدَمًا بِنَظْمٍ مُؤتَلِفٍ مُتَراكِبْ

(10) khalaqa mukhkhan wa ʿaẓman wa ʿaḍudan wa ʿurūqan wa laḥman wa jildan wa shaʿran wa daman bi-naẓmin mu'talifin mutarākib
(He) created the brain, bones, the upper arms, the veins, the flesh, the skin, the hair and the blood in an intricatly harmonious arrangement.

(11) مِنْ مَاءٍ دَافِقٍ يَخرُجُ مِنْ بَينِ الصُّلبِ وَالتَّرائِبْ

(11) min mā'in dāfiqin yakhruju min bayni 'ṣ-ṣulbi wa 't-tarā'ib
From a gushing fluid proceeding from between the backbone and the ribs.

(12) *(لاَ إلهَ إلاَّ الله) * كَريمٌ بَسَطَ لِخَلقِهِ بِسَاطَ كَرَمِهِ وَالمَوَاهِبْ

(12) <u>Lā ilāha illa 'l-Lāh</u>; Karīmun basaṭa li-khalqihi bisāṭa karamihi wa 'l-mawāhib
(There is no god but Allāh) the Generous. Who spreads over His creations a carpet of generosityand granted favors.

(13) يَنْزِلُ فِي كُلِّ لَيْلَةٍ إِلَى السَّمَاءِ الدُّنيَا وَيُنَادِيْ هَلْ مِنْ مُسْتَغفِرٍ هَلْ مِنْ تَائِبْ * (تَآئِبُونَ إِلَى اللهِ) *

(13) yanzilu fī kulli laylatin ila 'ṣ-samā'i 'd-dunyā wa yunādī hal min mustaghfirin hal min tā'ib. Tā'ibūna ila 'l-Lāh!

Descending every night to the lower heaven and calling out: "Is there anyone asking for forgiveness? Is there anyone seeking repentance?" (We seek repentance to Allāh).

(14) هَلْ مِنْ طَالِبِ حَاجَةٍ فَأُنِيلَهُ المَطَالِبْ

(14) Hal min ṭālibi ḥājatin fa-unīluhu 'l-maṭālib

"Is there anyone has any need; so that I may fulfil his need?"

(15) فَلَوْ رَأَيتَ الخُدَّامَ قِيَامًا عَلَى الأَقْدَامِ وَقَدْ جَادُوا بِالدُّمُوعِ السَّوَاكِبْ

(15) fa law ra'aita 'l-khuddāma qiyāman 'alā 'l-aqdāmi wa qad jādū bi 'd-dumū 's-sawākib

Would it not be good if you see those who serve standing and crying in front (of Your Lord)?

(16) وَالقَومَ بَينَ نَادِمٍ وَتَائِبٍ

(16) wa 'l-qawma bayna nādimin wa tā'ib

And (they) are standing in the state between remorse and repentance.

(17) وخَائِفٍ لِنَفسِهِ يُعَاتِبْ

(17) wa khā'ifin li-nafsihi yu'ātib

And (they) fear for themselves and thus they reprimand themselves

(18) وَآبِقٍ مِنَ الذُّنُوبِ إِلَيهِ هَارِبْ

(18) wa 'ābiqin mina 'dh-dhunūbi ilayhi hārib

And (they) run from their sins towards God.

(19) فَلاَ يَزَالُونَ فِيْ الاِسْتِغفَارِ حَتَّىْ يَكُفَّ كَفُّ النَّهَارِ ذُيُولَ الغَيَاهِبْ

(19) falā yazalūna fīl-istighfāri ḥattā yakuffa kafu 'n-nahāri dhuyūla 'l-ghayāhib

And they remain in this state of seeking forgiveness until daylight chases away darkness (until the morning).

(20) فَيَعُودُونَ وَقَدَ فَازُوْا بِالمَطْلُوْبِ وَأَدْرَكُوْا رِضَىْ المَحْبُوبِ وَلَمْ يَعُدْ أَحَدٌ مِنَ القَومِ وَهُوَ خَائِبْ

(20) fa ya'ūdūna wa qad fāzū bi 'l-maṭlūbi wa adrakū riḍā 'l-maḥbūb wa lam ya'ud aḥadun mina 'l-qawmi wa huwa khā'ib
And so they will return, after having successfully achieved their aims, and of having attained the pleasure of the Beloved; and not one man amongst them would have returned disappointed.

(21) ﴿ لاَ إِلَهَ إلاَّ الله ﴾ ٭ فَسُبْحَانَهُ تَعَالَىْ مِنْ مَلِكٍ أَوْجَدَ نُوْرَ نَبِيِّهِ مُحَمَّدٍ ﷺ مِنْ نُورِهِ قَبْلَ أَنْ يَخلُقَ آدَمَ مِنَ الطِّينِ اللَّازِبْ

(21) Lā ilāha illa 'l-Lāh! Fa-subḥānahu ta'ālā min malikin awjada nūra nabiyyihi Muḥammadin ṣalla 'l-Lāhu 'alaihi wa Sallama min nūrihi qabla an yakhluqa 'Ādama mina 'ṭ-ṭīni 'l-lāzib
(There is no God but Allāh) Glory to Allāh, Exalted is He, Who created the Light of His Prophet Muḥammad ﷺ from His Light, before He created Adam from clay.

(22) وَعَرَضَ فَخْرَهُ عَلَىْ الأَشْيَاءِ وَقَالَ هَذَا سَيِّدُ الأَنْبِيَاءِ وَأَجَلُّ الأَصْفِيَاءِ وَأَكْرَمُ الْحَبَايِبْ ٭

(22) wa 'arada fakhrahu 'alā 'l-ashyā'i wa qāla hādhā sayyidu 'l-anbiyā'i wa ajallu 'l-aṣfīyā'i wa 'akramu 'l-ḥabā'ib.
And God Then presented the Pride of His creation before all other things created and said, " This is the master of all the prophets, the most honored of all the chosen people and the most honored amongst those I love."

اللهُمَّ صَلِّ وَسَلِّمْ وَبَارِكْ عَلَيْهِ وَعلَىْ آلِه

Allāhuma ṣalli wa sallim wa bārik 'alayhi wa 'alā ālih

5 – Who is He?

(23) قِيلَ هُوَ آدَمُ *(عَلَيْهِ السَّلامْ)* قَالَ آدَمُ بِهِ أُنِيلُهُ أَعْلَى الْمَرَاتِبْ

(23) Qīla huwa 'Ādam ('alayhi 's-salām!), qāla 'Ādamu bihi 'unīluhu ''lā 'l-marātib;

(After Allāh showed the Light of Muḥammad ﷺ in Heaven), then the Angels asked "Is it Adam ﷺ?" (Allāh) said: "Because of him, I will grant Adam a high status."

(24) قِيلَ هُوَ نُوحٌ *(عَلَيْهِ السَّلامْ)* قَالَ نُوحٌ بِهِ يَنْجُو مِنَ الْغَرَقِ وَيَهْلَكُ مَن خَالَفَهُ مِنَ الأَهْلِ وَالأَقَارِبْ

(24) qīla huwa Nūḥ ('alayhi 's-salām!) qāla Nūḥun bihi yanjū mina 'l-gharaqi wa yahlaku man khālafahu mina 'l-'ahli wa 'l-'aqārib

(The angels asked): "Is it Nūḥ ﷺ?" (Allāh) said: "Because of him, Nūḥ Will be saved from drowning in his ark, while whoever disobeyed him be it family or relatives will perish."

(25) قِيلَ هُوَ إِبْرَاهِيمُ *(عَلَيْهِ السَّلامْ)* قَالَ إِبْرَاهِيمُ بِهِ تَقُومُ حُجَّتُهُ عَلَى عُبَّادِ الأَصْنَامِ وَالْكَوَاكِبْ

(25) qīla huwa 'Ibrāhīm ('alayhi 's-salām!); qāla 'Ibrāhīmu bihi taqūmu ḥujjatuhu 'alā 'ubbadi 'l-aṣnāmi wa 'l-kawākib

(The angels asked): "Is it Abraham ﷺ?" (Allāh) said: "Because of him Abraham is able to make his case against the worshipers of idols and stars."

(26) قِيلَ هُوَ مُوسَى *(عَلَيْهِ السَّلامْ)* قَالَ مُوسَى أَخُوهُ وَلَكِنَّ هَذَا حَبِيْبٌ وَمُوسَى كَلِيمٌ وَمُخَاطَبْ

(26) qīla huwa Mūsā ('alayhi 's-salām!) qāla Mūsā akhūhu wa lākinna hādhā ḥabībun wa Mūsā kalīmun wa mukhāṭib

(The angels asked): "Is it Moses ﷺ?" (Allāh) said: "Moses is his brother, but he is the beloved one of Allāh, while Moses only conversed with Allah."

(27) قِيلَ هُوَ عِيسَى *(عَلَيْهِ السَّلَام)* قَالَ عِيسَى يُبَشِّرُ بِهِ وَهُوَ بَيْنَ يَدَيْ نُبُوَّتِهِ كَالْحَاجِبْ

(27) qīla huwa 'Īsā ('alayhi 's-salām!); qāla 'Īsā yubash-shiru bihi wa huwa bayna yaday nubwwatihi ka 'l-ḥājib

(The angels asked): "Is it Jesus ?" (Allāh) said: "Jesus only brought the good news of his Prophethood. Jesus is like a veil before his prophethood."

(28) قِيلَ فَمَنْ هَذَا الْحَبِيبُ الْكَرِيمُ الَّذِي أَلْبَسْتَهُ حُلَّةَ الْوَقَارْ، وَتَوَّجْتَهُ بِتِيجَانِ الْمَهَابَةِ وَالافْتِخَارْ، وَنَشَرْتَ عَلَى رَأْسِهِ الْعَصَائِبْ

(28) qīla faman hādha 'l-ḥabību 'l-karīmu 'lladhī albastahu ḥullata 'l-waqār; Wa tawwajtahu bi tījāni 'l-mahābati wa 'l-iftikhār, wa nasharta 'alā ra'sihi 'l-'aṣā'ib

(The angels asked): "So who is this beloved and honored one whom you dressed with the dress of honor, and whom you crowned with the crown of a mighty presense and pride, and whom you placed upon his head many banners?

(29) قَالَ هُوَ نَبِيٌّ اِسْتَخَرْتُهُ مِنْ لُؤَيِّ بن غَالِبْ

(29) qāla huwa nabiyyuni 'istakhartuhu min lu'ayyi bni ghālib

(Allāh) said: He is the prophet whom I have chosen from the descendant of Lu'ayy ibn Ghālib".

(30) يَمُوتُ أَبُوهُ وَأُمُّهُ وَيَكْفُلُهُ جَدُّهُ ثُمَّ عَمُّهُ الشَّقِيقُ أَبُو طَالِبْ

(30) Yamūtu 'abūhu wa 'ummuhu wa yakfuluhu jadduhu thumma 'ammuhu 'sh-shaqīqu Abū Ṭālib!

His father and mother will pass away, he will then be looked after by his grandfather, then by his paternal uncle Abū Ṭālib.

اللهُمَّ صَلِّ وَسَلِّمْ وَبَارِكْ عَلَيْهِ وَعلَىٰ آلِه

Allāhuma ṣalli wa sallim wa bārik 'alayhi wa 'alā ālih

6 - The Prophet's Blessed Description

اللهُمَّ صَلِّ وَسَلِّمْ وَبَارِكْ عَلَيْهِ وَعلَىْ آلِه

Allāhuma ṣalli wa sallim wa bārik ʿalayhi wa ʿalā ālih

31) يُبْعَثُ مِنْ تِهَامَة ، بَيْنَ يَدي الْقِيَامَةْ ، فِيْ ظَهْرِهِ عَلامَةٌ ، تُظِلُّهُ الْغَمَامَةُ تُطِيعُهُ السَّحَائِبْ

(31) Yubʿathu min tihāmah, bayna yadayhi 'l-qiyāmah, fī ẓahrihi ʿalāmah, tuẓilluhu 'l-ghamāmah, tuṭīʿuhu 's-sahā'ib

He was raised among the people of Tihāma, right before the Day of Reckoning; on his back there is a mark; the clouds will give him shade, and the rain clouds will obey his command.

32) فَجْرِيُّ الْجَبِيْنِ لَيْلِيُّ الذَّوَآئِبْ

(32) Fajriyyu 'l-jabīni, layliyyu 'dh-dhawā'ib

His forehead shines like the light of dawn; his hair is dark like the night.

33) أَلِفِيُّ الأَنْفِ مِيْمِيُّ الْفَمِ نُونِيُّ الْحَاجِبْ

(33) Alfiyyu 'l-anfi, mīmiyyu 'l-fami, nūniyyu 'l-ḥājib

His nose is straight like the letter Alif, his mouth is round like the letter Mīm, and his eyebrows are shaped like the letter Nūn.

34) سَمْعُهُ يَسْمَعُ صَرِيْرَ الْقَلَمِ ، بَصَرُهُ إِلَى السَّبْعِ الطِّبَاقِ ثَاقِبْ

(34) Samʿuhu yasmaʿu ṣarīra 'l-qalami, baṣaruhu ila 's-sabʿi 't-ṭibāqi thāqib

His hearing can hear the scratching of the Pen (of power); his sight can penetrate all the way thru the seven heavens.

35) قَدَمَاهُ قَبَّلَهُمَا الْبَعِيرُ فَأَزَالَا مَا اشْتَكَاهُ مِنَ الْمِحَنِ وَالنَّوَآئِبْ

(35) Qadamāhu qabbalahumā 'l-baʿīru fa-azālā mashtakāhu mina 'l-miḥani wa 'n-nawā'ib

After the camel kissed his two feet, all the ailments and hardship which it complained to him of, were removed.

(36) آمَنَ بِهِ الْضَّبُّ وَسَلَّمَت عَلَيهِ الأَشْجَارُ وَخَاطَبَتْهُ الأَحْجَارُ وَحَنَّ إِلَيْهِ الْجِذْعُ حَنِينَ حَزِيْنٍ نَادِبْ

(36) 'Āmana bihi ḍ-ḍabbu wa sallamat 'alayhi 'l-ashjāru wa khāṭabat-hu 'l-aḥjāru wa ḥanna ilayhi 'l-jidh'u ḥaninā ḥazīnin nādib

The hyena stated it's faith in him, and the mimosa trees saluted him. The stones spoke to him. The stump of the date tree yearned for him such a yearning, which caused it to lament and moan with sorrow.

(37) يَدَاهُ تَظْهَرُ بَرَكَتُهُمَا فِيْ الْمَطَاعِمِ وَالْمَشَارِبْ

(37) Yadāhu taẓharu barakatuhumā fil-maṭā'imi wa 'l-mashārib

His two hands would manifest their blessings in the [increase of] food and drink they touch.

(38) قَلْبُهُ لا يَغْفُلُ وَلا يَنَامُ وَلَكِن لِلْخِدْمَةِ عَلَى الْدَّوَامِ مُرَاقِبْ

(38) Qalbuhu lā yaghfulu wa lā yanāmu wa lākin li 'l-khidmati 'ala 'd-dawāmi murāqib

His heart is never heedless and never sleeps; but rather it is always standing ready in [His Lord's] duty and service,

(39) إنْ أُوذِيَ يَعفُوْ وَلا يُعَاقِبْ

(39) 'In ūdhīya ya'fu wa lā yu'āqib

When he is harmed, he always forgives and he would never punish.

(40) وَإِنْ خُوصِمَ يَصْمُتُ وَلا يُجَاوِبْ

(40) Wa 'in khūṣima yaṣmutu wa lā yujāwib

When affronted he would keep silent and he would not respond.

(41) أَرْفَعُهُ إِلَى أَشْرَفِ الْمَرَاتِبْ

(41) 'Arfa'uhu ilā ashrafi 'l-marātib;

Allāh raised him to the highest station of honor.

(42) فِيْ رَكْبَةٍ لا تَنْبَغِيْ قَبْلَهُ وَلا بَعْدَهُ لِرَاكِبْ

(42) Fī rakbatin lā tanbaghī qablahu wa lā ba'dahu li-rākib

On a ride that no other traveler had ever experienced, before him or after him,

(43) فِيْ مَوْكِبٍ مِنَ الْمَلَائِكَةِ يَفُوْقُ عَلَى سَائِرِ الْمَوَاكِبْ

(43) Fī mawkibim-mina 'l-mala'ikati yafuqu ʿalā sā'iri 'l-mawākib
In the company of a delegation of angels that exceeds in honor all other delegations.

(44) فَإِذَا ارْتَقَى عَلَى الْكَوْنَيْنِ وَانْفَصَلَ عَنِ الْعَالَمَيْنِ كُنْتُ لَهُ أَنَا النَّدِيْمَ وَالْمُخَاطِبْ ۞

(44) Fa idhar- rtaqā ʿalā 'l-kawnayni, wa 'anfaṣala ʿani 'l-ʿalamayni wa waṣala ila qābi qawsayni kuntu lahu anā-n-nadīma wa 'l-mukhāṭib;
"When he reaches above the two universes, and seperates himself from the two worlds, at that time I will be his companion, and I will be the one who speaks to him."

اللهُمَّ صَلِّ وَسَلِّمْ وَبَارِكْ عَلَيْهِ وَعَلَىْ آلِه
Allāhuma ṣalli wa sallim wa bārik ʿalayhi wa ʿalā ālih

(45) ثُمَّ أَرُدُّهُ مِنَ الْعَرْشِ قَبْلَ أَنْ يَبْرُدَ الْفَرْشُ وَقَدْ نَالَ جَمِيعَ الْمَآرِبْ

(45) Thumma arudduhu mina 'l-ʿarsh, qabla an yabruda 'l-farsh, wa qad nāla jamīʿa 'l-mārib
After which I will bring him back from the Throne before his bed is cold. He would have then attained all his hearts desire.

(46) فَإِذَا شُرِّفَتْ تُرْبَةُ طَيْبَةَ مِنْهُ بِأَشْرَفِ قَالِبْ

(46) Fa'idhā shurrifat turbatu ṭaybata minhu bi ashrafi qālib
And when the soil of Ṭayyibah (Medina) became honored by the presense of his most honored form upon it

(47) سَعَتْ إِلَيْهِ أَرْوَاحُ الْمُحِبِّيْنَ عَلَى الأَقْدَامِ وَالنَّجَائِبْ

(47) Saʿat ilayhi arwāḥu 'l-muḥibbīn ʿalā 'l' aqdāmi wa 'n-najā'ib;
Then there ran to him the souls of every one who loved him, some walking while others riding the camels.

اللهُمَّ صَلِّ وَسَلِّمْ وَبَارِكْ عَلَيْهِ وَعَلَىْ آلِه
Allāhuma ṣalli wa sallim wa bārik ʿalayhi wa ʿalā ālih

7 - The Caravaner's Qaṣīda

(48) صَلاَةُ اللهِ مَا لاحَتْ كَوَاكِبْ عَلَى أَحْمَدْ خَيْرِ مَنْ رَكِبَ النَّجَائِبْ
(48) ṢalātulLāhi mā lāḥat kawākib
'alā Āḥmad khayri man rakiba 'n-najā'ib
Allāh's blessings on the number of stars in the sky;
Upon Ahmad, the best of those who rode the camels.

(49) حَدَى حَادِيْ السُّرَى بِاسْمِ الْحَبَائِبْ فَهَزَّ السُّكْرُ أَعْطَافَ الرَّكَائِبْ

(49) Ḥadā ḥādi ' surā bismi 'l-ḥabā'ib Fahazza 's-sukru 'a'ṭāfa 'r-rakā'ib

The camels Swayed drunk with love as they listened to the singer singing the name of the beloved;

(50) أَلَمْ تَرَهَا وَقَدْ مَدَّتْ خُطَاهَا وَسَالَتْ مِنْ مَدَامِعِهَا سَحَائِبْ

(50) Alam tarahā wa qad maddat khuṭāhā Wa sālat min madāmi'iha saḥā'ib

Did you not see how it (the camel in excitement) took longer steps and tears poured from its eyes with joy?

(51) وَمَالَتْ لِلْحِمَى طَرَباً وَحَنَّتْ إِلَى تِلْكَ الْمَعَالِمِ وَالْمَلاَعِبْ

(51) Wa mālat li 'l-ḥimā ṭaraban wa ḥannat Ilā tilka 'l-ma'ālimi wa 'l-malā'ib

It turned towards those sites with yearning; and longed for such places and playfields.

(52) فَدَّعْ جَذْبَ الزِمَامِ وَلاَ تَسُقْهَا فَقَائِدُ شَوْقِهَا لِلْحَيِّ جَاذِبْ

(52) Fada' jadhba 'z-zimāmi wa lā tasuqhā Faqā'idu shawqiha li 'l-ḥayyi jādhib

So stop pulling on the reins trying to drive the camels; for its yearning is the driver pulling it towards the living one.

(53) فهِمْ طَرَباً كَمَا هَامَتْ وَإلاَّ فَإنَّكَ فِيْ طَرِيْقِ الْحُبِّ كَاذِب

(53) Fahim ṭaraban kamā hāmat wa illā Fa innaka fī ṭarīqi 'l-ḥubbi kādhib

You must also be overtaken with the melody like the camels are; if you are not, then you are not sinsere in the path of love.

(54) أَمَاْ هَذَا الْعَقِيْقُ بَدَى وَهَذِى قِبَابُ الْحَيِّ لاَحَتْ وَالْمَضَارِبْ

(54) Amā hadha 'l-ʿaqiqu bada wa hādhi Qibābu 'l-ḥayyi lāḥat wa 'l-maḍārib

There, the sight of the village, al-ʿAqīq, can be seen; The sight of village housetops and tents.

(55) وَتِلْكَ الْقُبَّةُ الْخَضْرَا وَفِيْهَا نَبِيٌّ نُوْرُهُ يَجْلُوْ الْغَيَاهِبْ

(55) Wa tilka 'l-qubbatu 'l-khaḍrā wa fīhā Nabīyyun nūruhu yajlu 'l-ghayāhib

And there is the green dome; In it rests a Prophet whose light removes away darkness,

(56) وَقَدْ صَحَّ الرِّضَى وَدَنَا التَّلاَقِيْ وَقَدْ جَاءَ الْهَنَا مِنْ كُلِّ جَانِبْ

(56) Wa qad ṣahha 'r-riḍā wa danā 't-talāqi Wa qad jā 'al-hanā min kulli jānib

The plreasure have been achieved, as the meeting drew nearer, And happiness has arrived from all sides.

(57) فَقُلْ لِلنَّفْسِ دُونَكِ وَالتَّمَلِّيْ فَمَا دُونَ الْحَبِيْبِ الْيَوْمَ حَاجِبْ

(57) Fa qul li 'n-nafsi dūnaki wa 't-tamalli Famā dūna 'l-ḥabībi 'l-yawma ḥājib

Say to the self do not take your time; today anything other than the beloved is a veil.

(58) تَمَلَّيْ بِالْحَبِيْبِ بِكُلِّ قَصْدٍ فَقَدْ حَصَلَ الْهَنَا وَالْضِّدُّ غَائِبْ

(58) Tamallī bi 'l-ḥabībi bi kulli qasdin Fa qad ḥaṣala 'l-hanā waḍ-ḍaddu ghā'ib

Take your time when you are with the beloved; when happiness is reached and all else is abscent.

(59) نَبِيُّ اللهِ خَيْرُ الْخَلْقِ جَمْعاً لَهُ أَعْلَى الْمَنَاصِبِ وَالْمَرَاتِبْ

(59) Nabīyyullāhi khayru 'l-khalqi jam'an   Lahu 'a'lā 'l-manāṣibi wa 'l-marātib

The Prophet of Allah is the best of all creations; to him belongs the highest titles and stations.

(60) لَهُ الْجَاهُ الرَّفِيعُ لَهُ الْمَعَالِيْ   لَهُ الشَّرَفُ الْمُؤَبَّدُ وَالْمَنَاقِبْ

(60) Lahu 'l-jāhu 'r-rafi'u lahu 'l-ma'ālī   Lahu 'sh-sharafu 'l-mu'abbadu wa 'l-manāqib

He owns the highest esteem and high status; he owns the eternal honor and high rank.

(61) فَلَوْ أَنَّا سَعَيْنَا كُلَّ حِيْنٍ   عَلَى الأَحْدَاقِ لاَ فَوْقَ النَّجَائِبْ

(61) Falaw 'anna sa'aina kullu ḥīnin   'ala 'l'aḥdāqi lā fawqa 'n-najā'ib

If we walk every time (towards Medina) upon our eylashs, not on top of the camels

(62) وَلَوْ أَنَّا عَمِلْنَا كُلَّ يَوْمٍ   لأَحْمَدَ مَوْلِداً قَدْ كَانَ وَاجِبْ

(62) Wa law anna 'amilna kulla yawmin   Li 'Aḥmada mawlidan qad kāna wājib

And even if we perform every day the Mawlid celebration for Ahmad; we would only be doing our obligation.

(63) عَلَيْهِ مِنَ الْمُهَيْمِنِ كُلَّ وَقْتٍ   صَلاَةٌ مَا بَدَا نُوْرُ الْكَوَاكِبْ

(63) 'Alayhi mina 'l-muhaimini kulla waqtin   Ṣalātun mā badā nūru 'l-kawākib

In every moment he recieves blessings from the All Powerful one, for as long as the light of the stars shine.

(64) تَعُمُّ الآلَ وَالأَصْحَابَ طُرًّا   جَمِيْعَهُمُ وَعِتْرَتَهُ الأَطَايِبْ

(64) Ta'ummu 'l-āla wa 'l-aṣḥāba ṭurran   Jamī'ahum wa 'itratahu 'l-'aṭāyib

It covers all his family and companions; and all his goodness filled descendents.

اللهُمَّ صَلِّ وَسَلِّمْ وَبَارِكْ عَلَيْهِ وَعَلَى آلِه

Allāhuma ṣalli wa sallim wa bārik 'alayhi wa 'alā ālih

8 - Author's Praise

اللهُمَّ صَلِّ وَسَلِّمْ وَبَارِكْ عَلَيْهِ وَعَلَىْ آلِه
Allāhuma ṣalli wa sallim wa bārik ʿalayhi wa ʿalā ālih

فَسُبْحَانَ مَنْ خَصَّهُ ﷺ بِأَشْرَفِ الْمَنَاصِبِ وَالْمَرَاتِبْ *

Fa subḥāna man khaṣṣahu ṣallalLāhu ʿalayhi wa sallam bi ashrafi ʾl-manāṣibi wa ʾl-marātib;

Glory be to Allāh who excluisvely dignified him (pbuh) with the most honorable titles and stations.

أَحْمَدُهُ عَلَى مَا مَنَحَ مِنَ الْمَوَاهِبْ *

ʿAḥmaduhu ʿalā mā manaḥa mina ʾl-mawāhib;

I praise Allah for all the bountiful grants which he granted (to His prophet).

وَأَشْهَدُ أَنْ لآ إِلَهَ إِلاَّ اللهُ وَحْدَهُ لاَ شَرِيْكَ لَهُ رَبُّ الْمَشَارِقِ وَالْمَغَارِبْ *

Wa ashhadu an lā ilāha illa-Allāh waḥdahu lā sharīka lahu Rabbu ʾl-mashāriqi wa ʾl-maghārib;

And I bear witness that there is no God but Allāh, the One and Only, without partner, Lord of the Easts and the Wests;

وَأَشْهَدُ أَنَّ سَيِّدَنَا مُحَمَّداً عَبْدُهُ وَرَسُوْلُهُ الْمَبْعُوْثُ إِلَى سَائِرِ الأَعَاجِمِ وَالأَعَارِبْ *

Wa ashhadu anna sayyidana Muḥammadan ʿabduhu wa Rasūluhu ʾl-mabʿūthi ʾila sāʾiri ʾl-aʿājimi wa ʾl-aʿārib;

And I bear witness that our leader Muḥammad ﷺ is His servant and Messenger who was sent to both the non-Arabs and the Arabs.

صَلَّى اللهُ عَلَيْهِ وَسَلَّمَ وَعَلَى آلِهِ وَأَصْحَابِهِ أُوْلِي الْمَآثِرِ وَالْمَنَاقِبْ *

Ṣalla ʾl-Lāhu ʿalayhi wa sallama wa ʿala ālihi wa aṣḥābihi uli ʾl-maʾāthiri wa ʾl-manāqib;

May Allāh's blessings and salutations be upon him and his family and companions, owners of gloriously remembered deeds and history

صَلاةً وَسَلاَمَاً دَائِمَيْنِ مُتَلاَزِمَيْنِ يَأْتِي قَائِلُهُمَا يَوْمَ الْقِيَامَةِ غَيْرَ خَآئِبْ ۞

Ṣalātan wa salāman dā'imayni mutalāzimayni ya'ti qā'iluhumā yawma 'l-qiyyāmati ghayra khā'ib.

Continuous unending Blessings and Salutations; for whoever utters them will not be disappointed on the day of judgment.

اللهُمَّ صَلِّ وَسَلِّمْ وَبَارِكْ عَلَيْهِ وَعَلَىْ آلِه

Allāhuma ṣalli wa sallim wa bārik 'alayhi wa 'alā ālih

9 - His Pure Ancestry

اللهُمَّ صَلِّ وَسَلِّمْ وَبَارِكْ عَلَيْهِ وَعَلَىْ آلِه

Allāhuma ṣalli wa sallim wa bārik ʿalayhi wa ʿalā ālih

(1) أَوَّلُ مَا نَستَفتِحُ بإِيرَادِ حَدِيثَينِ وَرَدَا فِيْ نَبيٍّ كَانَ قَدْرُهُ عَظِيمًا ❊ وَنَسَبُهُ كَرِيمًا ❊ وَصِرَاطُهُ مُستَقِيمًا

(1) Awwalu mā nastaftiḥu bi-ʾirādi ḥadīthaini waradā fī Nabiyyin kāna qadruhu ʿāẓīmā; Wa nasabuhu karīma, wa ṣirāṭuhu mustaqīma

We begin this Mawlid with two narrations about a Prophet who possessed an inestimable greatness, an honorable ancestory and a path which is straight.

(2) قَالَ فِيْ حَقِّهِ مَنْ لَمْ يَزَلْ سَمِيعًا عَلِيمًا. إِنَّ اللهَ وَمَلآئِكَتَهُ يُصَلُّونَ عَلَى النَّبِيْ يَا أَيُّهَا الَّذِيْنَ آمَنُوْا صَلُّوا عَلَيْهِ وَسَلِّمُوْا تَسْلِيمًا ❊

(2) Qāla fī ḥaqqihi man lam yazal Samīʿan ʿAlīmā: Inna-Allāha wa malāʾikatahu yuṣallūna ʿalā ʾn-Nabiyyi yā ayyuhā ʾl-ladhīnā ʾamanu ṣallū ʿalayhi wa sallimū taslīma!

Allāh, the all-Hearing, and all-Knowing, said with regards to him ﷺ: "Allāh and His Angels send blessings upon the Prophet. O you who believe! Send your blessings on him, and salute him with all respect."

اللهُمَّ صَلِّ وَسَلِّمْ وَبَارِكْ عَلَيْهِ وَعَلَىْ آلِه

Allāhuma ṣalli wa sallim wa bārik ʿalayhi wa ʿalā ālih

(3) الْحَدِيثُ الأَوَّلُ عَنْ بَحْرِ الْعِلمِ الْدَّافِقِ، وَلِسَانِ الْقُرْآنِ الْنَّاطِقْ، أَوْحَدِ عُلَمَاءِ الْنَّاسِ، سَيِّدِنَا عَبدُ اللّهِ ابْنِ سَيِّدِنَا العَبَّاسْ رَضِيَ اللّهُ عَنهُمَا، عَنْ سَيِّدِنَا رَسُولِ اللّهِ ﷺ أَنَّهُ قَالْ: إنَّ قُرَيشاً كَانَتْ نُوْرًا بَينَ يَدَيْ اللّه عزَّ وَجَلَّ قبلَ أَنْ يَخلُقَ آدَمَ عَلَيهِ الْسَّلامُ بِأَلفَيْ عَامٍ، يُسَبِّحُ اللّهَ ذَلِكَ النُورُ وَتُسَبِّحُ الْمَلآئِكَةُ بِتَسْبِيحِهْ.
فَلَمَّا خَلَقَ اللّهُ آدَمَ عَلِيهِ السَّلامُ أَودَعَ ذَلِكَ النُورَ فِي طِينَتِه

(3) (Al-ḥadīthu 'l-awwalu) 'an baḥri 'l-'ilmi 'd-dāfiqi, wa lisāni 'l-qur'ānin nāṭiq, awḥadi 'ulamā'i 'n-nās, Sayyidinā 'Abdillāh ibni Sayyidinā 'l-'Abbās raḍīya-Allāhu 'anhumā 'an RasūlilLāhi ṣallallāhu 'alayhi wa sallama annahu qāl, inna Qurayshan kānat nūran baynā yadayi 'l-Lāhi 'azza wa jalla qabla an yakhluqa 'Ādama 'alayhi's-salām bi alfay 'ām yusabbiḥu 'l-Lāha dhālika'n-nūru wa tusabbiḥu 'l-mala'ikatu bi tasbiḥih, falammā khalaqa 'l-Lāhu 'Ādama 'alayhi's-salām awda'a dhālika'n-nūra fī ṭīnatih.

The first Hadith was narrated from the gushing forth ocean of knowledge, the speaking tongue of the quran, the unique scholar amongst all people, our leader, 'Abdullāh ibn 'Al- Abbās, may Allāh bless him and his father, who narrated from the Messenger of Allāh ﷺ, "Verily, the Quraysh was the light chosen by Allāh ﷻ before He created Adam by two thousand years. That Light (spirit [*ruh]* of Muḥammad ﷺ) glorified Allāh ﷻ and the angels also glorified Allāh ﷻ following it. When Allāh ﷻ created Adam, He deposited that light in the mud from which Adam ؑ. Was created"

(4) قَالَ ﷺ فَأَهبَطَنِيَ اللّهُ عزَّ وَجَلَّ [3] فِيْ ظَهرِ آدَمَ عَليهِ السَّلامْ

(4) qāla ṣalla 'l-Lāhu 'alayhi wa sallam fa'aḥbaṭaniya 'l-Lāhu 'azza wa jalla ila 'l-arḍi fī ẓahri 'Ādam 'alayhi's-salām

(Messenger of Allāh ﷺ) said, "So Allāh sent down my light to the face of the earth in the loins of Adam ؑ."

(5) وَحَمَلنِي فِي الْسَّفِينَةِ فِي صُلْبِ نُوحٍ عَلَيهِ السَّلامُ

(5) wa ḥamalanī fi 's-safīnati fī ṣulbi Nūḥin 'alayhi's-salām

"And it was carried in the loins of Nūḥ ؑ when he was on the ark."

(6) وَجَعَلَنِي فِي صُلبِ الْخَلِيلِ إبرَاهِيمَ عَلَيهِ السَّلامُ حِينَ قُذِفَ بِهِ فِي النَّارِ

(6) wa jaʿalānī fī ṣulbi ʾl-khalīl ʾIbrāhīma ʿalayhiʾs-salām hīnā qudhifa bihi fī ʾn-nār

"And he put me in the loins of Ibrahim ﷺ when he was thrown in the fire."

(7) وَلَمْ يَزَلِ اللهُ عزَّ وَجَلَّ يَنقُلُنِي مِنَ الأَصْلابِ الطَّاهِرَةِ إلَى الأَرحَامِ الزَّكِيَّةِ الفَاخِرَةِ، حَتَّىْ أَخْرَجَنِيَ اللهُ مِنْ بَينِ أَبَوَيَّ وَهُمَا لَمْ يَلتَقِيَا عَلَى سِفَاحٍ قَطّ!

(7) wa lam yazali ʾl-Lāhu ʿazza wa jalla yanqulunī mina ʾl-aṣlābi ʾṭ-ṭāhirati, ilaʾl-arḥami ʾz-zakiyyati ʾl-fākhirati ḥattā akhrajania ʾl-Lāhu min bayni abawayya wa humā lam yaltaqiyā ʿalā sifāḥin qaṭṭ.

"In this mannerw Allāh kept on movin me from noble loins into pure wombs, until Allāh brought me out from between my two parents, and neither of them ever committed fornication, whatsoever!"

اللهُمَّ صَلِّ وَسَلِّمْ وَبَارِكْ عَلَيْهِ وَعلَىْ آلِه

Allāhuma ṣalli wa sallim wa bārik ʿalayhi wa ʿalā ālih

10 - The Biblical Prediction of the Prophetic Kingdom

اللهُمَّ صَلِّ وَسَلِّمْ وَبارِكْ عَلَيْهِ وَعلَىْ آلِه

Allāhuma ṣalli wa sallim wa bārik ʿalayhi wa ʿalā ālih

(8) اَلحَدِيثُ الثَّانِيْ عَنْ عَطَاءِ بِن يَسَارٍ عَنْ كَعبِ الأَحبَارِ، قَالَ عَلَّمَنِي أَبِي التَّورَاةَ إلاَّ سِفرًا وَاحِدًا كَانَ يَختِمُهُ وَيُدخِلُهُ الصُندُوقْ

(8) Al-ḥadīthuth-thānī ʿan ʿAṭā'I bni Yasārin, ʿan Kaʿbi 'l-'Ahbār, qāla ʿallamanī abī a 't-tawrāta illa sifran wāḥidan kāna yakhtimuhu wa yudkhiluhu 'ṣ-ṣundūq

This second hadith was related by Ataʿa ibn Yassār from Kaʿabil Aḥbār. He said, "My father taught me the Book of Torah, except for one section from the book which he used to seal and lock away in a box".

(9) فَلَمَّا مَاتَ أَبِيْ فَتَحتُهُ فَإذَا فِيهِ نَبِيٌّ يَخرُجُ آخِرَ الزَمَانِ مَولِدُهُ بِمَكَّةَ، وَهِجَرَتُهُ بِالمَدِينَةِ، وَسُلطَانُهُ بِالشَامِ

(9) falammā māta 'abī fataḥtuhu fa'idhā fīhi Nabiyyun yakhruju ākhira 'z-zamān, mawliduhu bi Makkata, wa hijratuhu bi 'l-Madinah, wa sulṭānuhu bi 'sh-Shām.

"When my father passed away I opened the box and I read that section. It said, 'a Messenger will come at the end of time, he will be born in Mecca and he will emigrate to Medina, his kingship will be in Damascus."

(10) يَقُصُّ شَعرَهُ وَيَتَّزِرُ عَلَى وَسَطِهِ، يَكُونُ خَيرَ الأَنبِيَاءِ وَأُمَّتُهُ خَيرَ الأُمَمْ، يُكَبِّرُونَ اللهَ تَعَالَىْ عَلَىْ كُلِّ شَرْفٍ، يَصُفُّونَ فِيْ الصَلاَةِ كَصُفُوفِهِمْ فِيْ القِتَالْ، قُلُوبُهُمْ مَصَاحِفُهُمْ، يَحْمَدُونَ اللهَ تَعَالَىْ عَلَىْ كُلِّ شِدَّةٍ وَرخَاءْ، ثُلُثٌ يَدخُلُونَ

(10) yaquṣṣu shaʿrahu wa yattaziru ʿalā wasaṭihi yakunu khayra 'l-anbiyā'i wa ummatuhu khayra 'l-'umam, yukabbiruna 'l-Lāh taʿalā ʿalā kulli sharafin yaṣuffūna fīṣ-ṣalāti ka ṣufūfihim fi 'l-qitāl, qulūbuhum maṣāḥifuhum yaḥmadūna 'l-Lāha taʿalā ʿalā kulli shiddatin wa rakhā',

"He will cut his hair and he will wraps a cloth around his waist." He will the best amongst the prophets, and his nation will the best amongst nation. They glorify Allāh for every honor bestowed on them. They will keep straight rows during their prayers just as they will do in battle. Their hearts are are their books and they thank Allāh in every condition whether in difficulty or ease."

(11)الْجَنَّةَ بِغَيْرِ حِسَابْ! *(اللهُمَّ اجْعَلْنَا مِنْهُمْ)*

وَثُلُثٌ يَأْتُونَ بِذُنُوبِهِمْ وَخَطَايَاهُمْ فَيُغفَرُ لَهُمْ، وَثُلُثٌ يَأْتُونَ بِذُنُوبٍ وَخَطَايَا عِظَامْ

(11) thuluthun yadkhulūna 'l-jannata bi-ghayri ḥisāb; (Allāhummā 'jʿalnā minhum) Wa thuluthun ya'tūna bi-dhunūbihim wa khaṭāyāhum fa-yughfaru lahum, wa thuluthun yā'tūna bi-dhunūbin wa khaṭayā ʿiẓām,

"A third of them will enter heaven without their deeds being weighed. ("O Allāh, make us from among them.") And a third will arrive with sins and mistakes and they will be forgiven. And a third will arrive bearing heavy sins and grave mistakes."

(12) فَيَقُولُ اللهُ تَعَالَى لِلمَلآئِكَةِ اِذْهَبُوا فَزِنُوهُمْ، فَيَقُولُونَ رَبَّنَا وَجَدنَاهُمْ أَسرَفُوْا

عَلَىْ أَنفُسِهِمْ وَوَجدنَا أَعمَالَهُمْ مِنَ الذُّنُوبِ كَأَمثَالِ الجِبَالِ، غَيرَ أَنَّهُمْ يَشهَدُونَ

"أَنْ لآ إِلَهَ إِلاَّ اللهُ وَأَنَّ مُحَمَّدًا رَسُولُ اللهِ" صَلَّىْ اللهُ عَلَيهِ وَسَلَّمْ!

(12) fa yaqulu 'l-Lāhu taʿalā li 'l-malā'ikati 'dh-habu fa-zinūhum fa yaqulūna Rabbanā wajadnāhum asrafu ʿalā anfusihim; wa wajadnā aʿmalahum mina 'dh-dhunūbi ka amthāli 'l-jibāli ghayra annahum yashhadūna 'an lā ilāha illa 'l-Lāhu wa anna Muḥammadan Rasūlullāhi ṣallallāhu ʿalayhi wa sallam;

So Allāh will order the Angels: "O My angels go and weigh their deeds." The angels will say, "O our Lord, we find these people oppressed themselves and their sinful deeds are like mountains, except for their bearing witness that there is no god but Allāh and Muḥammad is the Messenger of Allāh ﷺ."

(أَشهَدُ أَنْ لآ إِلَهَ إِلاَّ اللهُ وَأَنَّ مُحَمَّدًا رَسُولُ اللهِ)

Ashhadu ʿan lā ʿilāha illa l-Lāhu wa ashhadu anna Muḥammadan Rasūlullāh.

I bear witness that there is no god but Allāh and I bear witness that Muḥammad is the Messenger of Allāh.

اللهُمَّ صَلِّ وَسَلِّمْ وَبارِكْ عَلَيْهِ وَعلىْ آلِه

Allāhuma ṣalli wa sallim wa bārik ʿalayhi wa ʿalā ālih

(13) فَيَقُولُ الْحَقُّ وَعِزَّتِي وَجَلالِيْ، لاَ جَعَلتُ مَنْ أَخلَصَ لِي بِالشَّهَادَةِ كَمَنْ كَذَّبَ بِيْ، ادْخِلُوهُمُ الجَنَّةَ بِرَحْمَتِي!

(13) Fa yaqulu 'l-ḥaqqu wa ʿizzatī wa jalāli, lā jaʿaltu man akhlaṣa li bi'sh-shahādati kamān kadhdhaba bī, adkhiluhumu 'l-jannata bi-raḥmatī,

So The Real one will say, "By My Honor and My Majesty, I will not make equal those who are sincere to Me by their witnessing My Oneness and those who denied my existance. Let them enter the Garden of Paradise by My Mercy."

(14) يَا أَعَزَّ جَوَاهِرِ العُقُودِ ۞ وَخُلاصَةَ إِكْسِيرِ سِرِّ الوُجُودِ، مَادِحُكَ قَاصِرٌ وَلَوْ جَاءَ بِبَذْلِ المَجهُودْ، وَوَاصِفُكَ عَاجِزٌ عَنْ وَصفِ مَا حَوَيْتَ مِنْ خِصَالِ الكَرَمِ وَالجُودْ

(14) yā aʿazza jawāhiri 'l-ʿuqūd, wa khulāṣata iksīri sirri 'l-wujūd; mādiḥuka qāṣirun wa law jā'a bi-badhli 'l-majhūd wa wāṣifuka ʿājizun ʿan ḥaṣri mā ḥawayta min khiṣāli 'l-karami wa 'l-jūd.

O most precious jewel amongst all jewels, and the utmost Elixir for the secrets of existence: Your praise falls short even with one's utmost effort. The one describing you is unable to describe all the traits of generosity and goodness which you possess.

(15) الكَوْنُ إِشَارَةٌ وَأَنتَ المَقصُودْ، يَا أَشرَفَ مَنْ نالَ المَقَامَ المَحمُودْ، وَجَاءَت رُسُلٌ مِن قَبلِكَ وَلَكِنَّهُمْ بِالرِفْعَةِ وَالعُلَىْ لَكَ شُهُوْدْ.

(15) Al-kawnu ishāratun, wa 'Anta 'l-maqsūd; Yā 'ashrafa man nāla 'l-maqāma 'l-maḥmūd; wa jā'at rusulun min qablika lākinnahum bi 'r-rifʿati wa 'l-ʿulā laka shuhūd.

This universe is an indication and you are its purpose. O most honorable one of all who had achieved the Station of Praise, there preceded you (many) messengers, but they are all witnesses to your exaltedness and high station.

اللهُمَّ صَلِّ وَسَلِّمْ وَبَارِكْ عَلَيْهِ وَعلَىْ آلِه

Allāhuma ṣalli wa sallim wa bārik ʿalayhi wa ʿalā ālih

11 - His Birth (Mawlid)

اللهُمَّ صَلِّ وَسَلِّمْ وَبارِكْ عَلَيْهِ وَعلَىْ آلِه ***Allāhuma ṣalli wa sallim wa bārik ʿalayhi wa ʿalā ālih***

(16) أَحْضِرُوْا قُلُوْبَكُمْ يَا مَعْشَرَ ذَوِي الأَلْبَابِ * حَتَىْ أَجْلُوا لَكُمْ عَرَائِسَ مَعَانِي أَجَلِّ الأَحْبَابْ * الْمَخْصُوْصِ بَأَشْرَفِ الأَلْقَابْ * الرَّاقِي إِلَى حَضْرَةِ الْمَلِكِ الْوَهَّابْ * حَتَى نَظَرَ إِلَى جَمَالِهِ بِلا سِتْرٍ وَلاْ حِجَابْ

(16) Aḥdhirū qulūbakum yā maʿshara dhawi ʿl'albāb; ḥattā ajluwa lakum ʿarā'isa maʿāni ajalli ʿl-ʿaḥbāb; Al-makhṣūṣi bi ʿashrafi ʿl-ʿalqāb; Ar-rāqi ila haḍrati ʿl-Maliki ʿl-Wahhāb; Ḥattā naẓara ila jamālihi bilā sitrin wa lā ḥijāb

Be present with your hearts, O possessors of deep understanding, whilst I present to you the qualities of the Most Beloved, who received the most honored titles, the Ascender to the Divine Presence of the King, until he looked to His Beauty without obstruction or veil.

(17) فَلَمَّا آنَ أَوَانُ ظُهُورِ شَمْسِ الرِسَالَةْ فِي سَمَاءِ الْجَلالَة * خَرَجَ مَرسُوْمُ الْجَلِيْلِ لِنَقِيبِ الْمَمْلَكَةِ جِبْرِيلْ

(17) Falamma ʿānna awānu ẓuhūri shamsi ʿr-risālah; fī samā'i ʿl-jalālah; Kharaja marsūmu ʿl-jalīli li-naqībi ʿl-mamlakati Jibrīl,

When the time arrived for the dawn of the sun of prophethood in the sky of majesty, it was directed by Allāh to Gabriel the chief of the kingdom,

(18) يَا جِبْرِيلُ نَادِ فِي سَائِرِ الْمَخْلُوقَاتِ * مِنْ أَهْلِ الأَرْضِ وَالْسَمَاوَاتِ * بِالْتَّهَانِي وَالْبِشَارَاتْ

(18) Yā Jibrīl nādī fi sā'iri ʿl-makhlūqāt; Min āhli ʿl-ʿarḍi wa ʿs-samāwāt, bit-tahāni wa ʿl-bishārāt

"O Gabriel, announce the good news to all creations, from among the dwellers of the earth and the heavens with my congratulations and good tidings."

(19) فَإِنَّ النُّورَ الْمَصُونَ وَالسِّرَّ الْمَكْنُونَ الَّذِي أَوْجَدْتُهُ قَبْلَ وُجُودِ الأَشْيَاءِ ۞
وَإِبْدَاعِ الأَرْضِ وَالسَّمَاءْ ۞ أَنْقُلُهُ إِلَى بَطْنِ أُمِّهِ مَسْرُورًا

(19) fa 'inna 'n-nūrra 'l-masūn, wa 's-sirra 'l-maknūn, 'lladhī awjadtuhu qabla wujūdi 'l-ashyā'i wa 'ibdā'i 'l-arḍi wa 's-samā'; Anquluhu fi hādhihi 'l-laylati ila baṭni ummihi masrūrā

"For the chosen light and the secret (of existence), which I created before the existence of all things and before the creation of the heavens and earth, on this night I move him to the womb of his mother happy"

(20) أَمْلأُ بِهِ الْكَوْنَ نُورًا ۞ وَأَكْفُلُهُ يَتِيمًا وَأُطَهِّرُهُ وَأَهْلَ بَيْتِهِ تَطْهِيرًا ۞

(20) Amla'u bihi 'l-kawna nūra, wa akfuluhu yatīman wa uṭahhiruhu wa 'ahla baytihi taṭ-hīra

"I fill this world with his light, support him in his orphanhood, and I purify him and his House with the utmost purification."

اللهُمَّ صَلِّ وَسَلِّمْ وَبَارِكْ عَلَيْهِ وَعَلَىٰ آلِه

Allāhuma ṣalli wa sallim wa bārik 'alayhi wa 'alā ālih

(21) فَاهْتَزَّ الْعَرْشُ طَرَبًا وَاسْتِبْشَارًا

(21) Fahtazza 'l-'arshu ṭaraban wa 'stibshārā

So the Throne shook with happiness and delight.

(22) وَازْدَادَ الْكُرْسِيُّ هَيْبَةً وَوَقَارًا

(22) Wazdāda 'l-kursīyyu haybatan wa waqāra

And the Footstool increased in magnificence and greatness.

(23) وَامْتَلأَتِ السَّمَاوَاتُ أَنْوَارًا ۞ وَضَجَّتِ الْمَلآئِكَةُ تَهْلِيلاً وَتَمْجِيدًا وَاسْتِغْفَارًا ۞

(23) Wamtala'ti 's-samāwātu anwārā; wa ḍajjati 'l-malā'ikatu tahlīlan wa tamjīdan wastighfārā;

The sky was filled with a brilliant light, and the voices of the angels vibrated with the recitation of God's Oneness, praising Him and seeking His forgiveness.

سُبْحَانَ اللهِ وَالْحَمْدُ لِلَّهْ وَلاَ إِلَهَ إِلاَّ اللهِ وَاللهُ أَكْبَرْ

(4 مرات)

Subḥāna 'l-Lāh wa 'l-ḥamdulillāh wa
Lā ilāha illa 'l-Lāh wa 'l-Lāhu akbar 3x

(24) وَلَمْ تَزَلْ أُمُّهُ تَرَى أَنْوَاعًا مِنْ فَخْرِهِ وَفَضْلِهِ إِلَى نِهَايَةِ تَمَامِ حَمْلِهْ

(24) Wa lam tazal 'ummuhu tarā 'anwā'an min fakhrihi wa faḍlihi ila nihāyati tamāmi ḥamlih

His mother continued to experience a variety of [signs of his] eminence and honor until the completion of her pregnancy

(25) فَلَمَّا اشْتَدَّ بِهَا الطَّلْقُ بِإِذْنِ رَبِّ الْخَلْقِ * وَضَعَتِ الْحَبِيْبَ صَلَّى اللهُ عَلَيْهِ وَسَلَّمَ سَاجِدًا شَاكِرًا حَامِدًا كَأَنَّهُ الْبَدْرُ فِيْ تَمَامِهْ * **(محل القيام)** *

(25) falammā 'shtadda bihā 'ṭ-ṭalqu, bi-idhni Rabbi 'l-khalqi wada'ati 'l-ḥabība ṣalla 'l-Lāhu 'alayhi wa sallama sājidan shākiran ḥāmidan ka 'annahu 'l-badru fī tamāmih; (stand up)

When the labor pains strengthened with the permission of Allāh (the Creator of All Creations), his mother gave birth to the beloved Prophet ﷺ in prostration thanking and praising Allāh as if he were the full moon in its splendor.

اللهُمَّ صَلِّ وَسَلِّمْ وَبَارِكْ عَلَيْهِ وَعلَىْ آلِه

Allāhuma ṣalli wa sallim wa bārik 'alayhi wa 'alā ālih

12 - His Youth

اللهُمَّ صَلِّ وَسَلِّمْ وَبَارِكْ عَلَيْهِ وَعلَى آلِه
Allaḥumma ṣalli wa sallim wa bārik ʿalāyh

(1) وَوُلِدَ صَلَّى اللهُ عَلَيْهِ وَسَلَّمَ مَختُونًا بيَدِ العِنايةِ

(1) Wulida ṣallal-Lahu ʿalayhi wa sallama makhtūnan biyadi 'l-ʿināyah,
The Prophet ﷺ was born already circumcised by the Hand of Care,

(2) مَكْحُولاً بِكُحل الهدايةِ

(2) Makḥullan bikuḥli 'l-hidāyah
His eyes lined with the kohl of guidance.

(3) فَأشرَقَ بِبَهائِهِ الفَضاءْ

(3) Fa-ashraqa bi-bahā'ihi 'l-faḍā',
The light of space rose through his splendor,

(4) وَتلألأَ الكَونُ مِنْ نُورِهِ وَأضاءْ

(4) Wa tal'la' 'l-kawnu min nūrihi wa aḍā'
And the cosmos was sparkling and shinning by his light

(5) وَدَخَلَ فِي عَهدِ بَيعَتِهِ مَنْ بَقِيَ مِنَ الخَلائِقِ كَمَا دَخَلَ فِيهَا مَن مَضَى

(5) Wa dakhala fī ʿahdi bayʿatihi man baqīya mina 'l-khalā'iqi kamā dakhala fihā man maḍā.
And whoever remained in this creation, gave the oath of allegiance to him, also those who came before.

(6) أوَّلُ فَضيلَةٍ مِنَ المُعجِزَاتِ بِخُمُودِ نَارِ فَارِسَ وَسُقُوطِ الشُّرُافَاتِ، وَرُمِيَتِ الشَيَاطِينُ مِنَ السَمَاءِ بالشُّهُبِ المُحرِقَاتْ، وَرَجَعَ كُلُّ جَبَّارٍ مِنَ الجِنِّ وَهُوَ بِصَولَةِ سَلطَنَتهِ ذَلِيلٌ خَاضِعٌ

(6) 'awwalu faḍilatin mina 'l-muʿjizāt bi-khumudi nāri fāris wa suqūṭi 'l-shurrufāt, wa rumiyati 'sh-shayaṭīnu mina 's-samā'i bi 'sh-shuhubi 'l-muḥriqāt, wa rajaʿa kullu jabbārin mina 'l-jinni wa huwa biṣawlati salṭanatihi dhalīlun khaḍiʿ
The first of the great miracles (announcing his coming) was when the fire of Persia died out (after 2000 years of burning continuosly), and its palaces' pavilion's collapsed. All the devils of the sky were pelted by the burning

meteors. Those jinn who had become mighty retreated, turned to disgrace and submission by the power of his sultanate,

(7) لَمَّا تَأَلَّقَ مِن سَناهُ النُورُ السَاطِعُ وَأَشرقَ مِن بَهائِهِ الضِّياءُ اللاَّمِعُ حَتَى عُرِضَ عَلَى المَرَاضِعْ

(7) Lamā ta'allaqa min sanāhu annūrus-sāṭi', wa'ashraqa min bahā'ihi 'l-ḍiyā'u lami' ḥatta 'uriḍa 'alāl-marāḍi'

When from his radiant presence came forth the shinning light, and from his splendor rose the illuminating brilliant shinning, until he was presented to the nursing mothers.

اللهُمَّ صَلِّ وَسَلِّمْ وَبَارِكْ عَلَيْهِ وَعلَىْ آلِه
Allahumma ṣalli wa sallim wa bārik 'alāyh

(8) قِيلَ مَن يَكْفُلُ هَذِهِ الدُرَّةَ اليَتيمَةَ التِي لا تُوجَدُ لَهَا قِيمَةٌ؟ قَالَتِ الطُيورُ: نَحنُ نَكْفُلُهُ وَنَغْتَنِمُ هِمَّتَهُ العَظِيْمَة

(8) Qīla: man yakfulu hadhihi 'd-durrata 'l-yatīmata 'llatī lā tūjad lahā qīmah? qālati 'ṭ-ṭuyūr: naḥnu nakfuluhu wa naghtanimu himmatahu 'l-'aẓīmah.

They asked, "Who will be the guardian of this unique orphaned Gem, which is priceless?" All the birds said, "We will support him and seize this opportunity to realize this great aspiration."

(9) قَالَتِ الوُحُوشُ: نَحنُ أولَىْ بذَلِكَ لِكَيْ نَنَالَ شَرَفهُ وَتَعظِيمَهْ

(9) Qālati 'l-wuhūsh: naḥnu awlā bi-dhālik likay nanāla sharafahu wa ta'ẓīmah.

The wild beasts said, "We have the first rights and are more suited so that we receive his honor and glorification."

(10) قِيلَ: يَا مَعشَرَ الأُمَمِ اسْكُنُوا فإنَّ اللهَ قَدْ حَكَمَ فِيْ سَابِق حِكْمَتِهِ القَدِيْمَةْ، بِأنَّ نَبِيَّهُ مُحَمَّداً صَلَّى اللهُ عَلَيْهِ وَسَلَّمَ يَكون رَضِيعًا لِحَلِيمَةَ الحَلِيمَةْ

(10) Qīla: yā ma'shara 'l-umami 'skunū fa-innal-Lāha qad ḥakama fī sābiqi ḥikmatihi 'l-qadīmah, bi-anna nabīyyahu Muḥammadan yakūnu raḍī'an li-Ḥalimata 'l-ḥalīmah.

Then it was said, "O company of nations, calm down, verily— Allah with his wisdom has determined that the Prophet Muḥammad will have Ḥalīmah the tender one, as his nursing mother."

اللهمَّ صَلِّ وَسَلِّمْ وَبَارِكْ عَلَيْهِ وَعلَىٰ آلِه
Allaḥumma ṣalli wa sallim wa bārik ʿalāyh

(11) فَلَمَّا أعرَضَ عَنهُ مَرَاضِعُ الإنسِ لِمَا سَبَقَ فِي طَيِّ الغَيبِ مِنَ السَّعَادَةِ لِحَلِيمَةَ بِنتِ أَبِي ذُؤَيبْ

(11) Fa-lammā aʿraḍa ʿanhu marāḍiʿu ʾl-insi limā sabaqa fī ṭayyi ʾl-ghayb mina ʾs-saʿādah li-Ḥalimata binti Abī Dhuʾayb.

And as it was decreed in the unseen world that such happiness was for Ḥalīmah binti Abī Dhūʾayb , all the (other) human wetnurses turned away from him.

(12) فَلَمَّا وَقَعَ نَظَرُهَا عَلَيْهِ، بَادَرَتْ مُسْرِعَةً إِلَيهِ، وَوَضَعَتْهُ فِيْ حِجْرِهَا، وَضَمَّتهُ إِلَى صَدْرِهَا

(12) Fa-lammā waqaʿa naẓaruhā ʿalayhi badarat musriʿatan ilayhi wa waḍaʿat-hu fī ḥijrihā wa ḍammaṭ-hu ila ṣadrihā.

When she saw him, she quickly took ran to him, she placed him ﷺ on her lap, and cuddld him to her chest.

(13) فَهَشَّ لهَا مُتَبَسِّمًا فَخَرَجَ مِن ثَغْرِهِ نُورٌ لَحِقَ بالسَّمَاءِ، فَحَمَلَتْهُ إِلَى رَحلِهَا، وَارتَحَلَتْ بِهِ إِلَى أَهلِهَا

(13) Fahash-shā lahā mubtassiman fakharaja min thaghrihi nūrun laḥiqa bi ʾs-samāʾi fa-ḥamalathu ila raḥlihā wa ʾartaḥalat bihi ila āhlihā.

A smile appeared on his face for her; a radiant light shone forth from his mouth and rose up to the heavens. She then took him ﷺ to her caravan and they went back to her family.

(14) فَلَمَّا وَصَلَتْ بِهِ إِلى مُقَامِهَا، عَايَنَتْ بَركَتَهُ حَتَّىْ عَلَى أَغنَامِهَا

(14) Fa-lammā waṣalat bihi ilā muqāmihā ʿāyanat barakatahu ḥatta ʿalā aghnāmihā.

When she arrived with him at her dewelling place, she noticed that effects of his blessings on her sheep.

(15) وَكَانَتْ كُلَّ يَومٍ تَرَى مِنهُ بُرهَانًا، وَتَرفَعُ لَهُ قَدرًا وَشَأنًا

(15) Wa kānat kulla yawmin tarā minhu burhānan wa tarfaʿu lahu qadran wa shāʾnā.

Then every day she noticed the signs of his superiority and greatness, as his status in her eye continued to increase.

(16) حَتَّى انْدَرَجَ فِي حُلَّةِ اللُّطفِ وَالاَمَانْ، وَدَخَلَ بَيْنَ إِخْوَتِهِ مَع الصِّبْيَانْ

(16) Ḥattā indarajā fī ḥullati 'l-luṭf wa 'l-amān wa dakhala bayna ikhwatihi māʿaṣ-ṣibyān.

Always in the custody of Allāh's ﷻ gentleness and safeguard; then he grew up and mixed with his foster-siblings and other children.

> اللهُمَّ صَلِّ وَسَلِّمْ وَبَارِكْ عَلَيْهِ وَعَلَىٰ آلِه
> *Allahumma ṣalli wa sallim wa bārik ʿalāyh*

(17) فَبَيْنَمَا الحَبِيبُ صَلَّى اللهُ عَلَيْهِ وَسَلَّمَ ذَاتَ يَومٍ نَاءٍ عَنِ الأوطَان، إِذْ أَقْبَلَ عَلَيهِ ثَلاثَةُ نَفَرٍ، كَأَنَّ وُجُوهَهُمُ الشَّمْسُ وَالقَمَر

(17) Fa-baynamā 'l-ḥabību ṣalla-Llāhu ʿalayhi wa sallam dhāta yawmin nā'in ʿani 'l-awṭān idh aqbala ʿalāyhi thalathatu nafarin ka'anna wujūhahumu 'sh-shamsu wa 'l-qamar.

One day, when the Beloved ﷺ was far from his home, there suddenly appeared three persons, their faces lit up like the moon and the sun.

(18) فَانْطَلَقَ الصِّبْيَانُ هَرَبًا، وَوَقَفَ النَّبِيُّ صَلَّى اللهُ عَلَيهِ وَسَلَّمَ مُتَعَجِّبًا

(18) Fa-anṭalaqa 'ṣ-ṣibyānu haraban wa waqafa 'n-nabiyyu ṣalla-Llāhu ʿalāyhi wa sallam mutaʿajjibā.

The other children dashed away, while the Prophet ﷺ stood by astonished.

(19) فَأَضْجَعُوهُ عَلَى الأرضِ إِضْجَاعًا خَفِيفًا، وَشَقُّوا بَطنَهُ شَقًّا لَطِيفًا

(19) Fa-aḍjaʿūhu ʿalā 'l-arḍi iḍjāʿan khafīfan wa shaqqū baṭnahu shaqqan laṭīfan.

Then they laid him on the ground gently and cut open his chest with a delicate incision.

(20) ثُمَّ أَخْرَجُوا قَلْبَ سَيِّدِ وَلَدِ عَدنَانَ، وشَرَحُوهُ بِسِكِّينِ الإحسَانِ، وَنَزَعُوا مِنهُ حَظَّ الشَيطَانِ، وَمَلأُوهُ بِالحِلمِ وَالعِلمِ وَاليَقِين وَالرضوَان

(20) Thumma akhrajū qalba sayyidi waladi ʿAdnāna wa sharaḥūhu bi sikkīni 'l-iḥsān wa nazaʿū minhu ḥaẓẓa 'sh-shayṭān wa mala'ūhu bi 'l-ḥilmi wa 'l-ʿilmi wa 'l-yaqīni wa 'l-riḍwān.

They then took out the heart of this "leader of the descendants of Adnan", they cut it open with the knife of moral excellence, they removed from it the share belonging to Satan, and they filled it up with patience, knowledge, faith, certainty, and contentment.

(21) وَأعَادُوهُ إلى مَكانِهِ فقامَ الحَبيبُ صَلَّى اللهُ عَليهِ وَسَلَّمَ سَوِيًّا كَمَا كَانَ

(21) Wa 'aʿadūhu ila makānihi fa-qāma 'l-ḥabību ṣalla-Llāhu ʿalāyhi wa sallam sawiyyan kamā kān.

Then they returned his heart to its original place. The Beloved ﷺ stood up comlete as he was before.

اللهُمَّ صَلِّ وَسَلِّمْ وَبَارِكْ عَلَيْهِ وَعلىْ آلِه
Allaḥumma ṣalli wa sallim wa bārik ʿalāyh

(22) فقَالَتِ المَلآئِكَةُ: يَا حَبيبَ الرَّحمَن، لَو عَلِمتَ مَا يُرادُ بِكَ مِنَ الخَير، لعَرَفتَ قَدرَ مَنزِلَتِكَ عَلى الغَير، وَازدَدتَ فَرحًا وَسُرورًا وَبهجَةً وَنُورًا

(22) Fa-qālati 'l-malā'ikatu: yā ḥabība 'r-raḥmān law ʿalimta mā yurādu bika mina 'l-khayr la-ʿarafta qadra manzilatika ʿalā 'l-ghayr wa azdadta faraḥan wa surūran wa bahjatan wa nūrā.

The three angels then said to him: "O the beloved of the Most Merciful Lord, if you knew what was planned for you of goodness, then you will know your status amongst other people. You would increase your joy and happiness, be delightful and radiant."

(23) يَا مُحَمَّدُ أبْشِرْ، فَقدْ نُشِرَتْ فِي الكَائنَاتِ أعلامُ عُلومِك، وَتبَاشَرَتِ المَخلوقَاتُ بِقُدومِكَ، وَلمْ يَبقَى شَيءٌ مِمَّا خَلَقَ اللهُ تَعالَى إلاَّ جَاءَ لأمرِكَ طَائِعاً، وَلِمَقَالَتِكَ سَامِعاً

(23) Yā Muḥammadu abshir faqad nushirat fi 'l-kā'ināti 'aʿlāmu ʿulūmik wa tabāsharati 'l-makhlūqāt bi-qudūmik wa lam yabqā sha'yun mimmā khalaqa 'Llāhu taʿālā illā jā'a li amrika ṭā'iʿan wa li-maqālatika sāmiʿā.

"O Muḥammad! Rejoice, for the knowledge of your coming was spread amongst the 'flag bearers of creation. Every creature will rejoice at your arrival. Every creation of Allah, the Exalted, will come to acknowledge your leadership, obey your orders, and listen to your speech."

(24) فَسيَأتِيكَ البَعيرُ بِذِمامِكَ يَستَجيرُ، وَالضَّبُّ وَالغَزالَةُ، يَشهدانِ لكَ بالرِّسَالةْ

(24) Fa-saya'tīka 'l-baʿīr bi-dhimāmika yastajīr, wa 'ḍ-ḍabu wa 'l-ghazālah yash-hadāni laka bi 'r-risālah.

"And the camel will come to you, asking for help and seeking your protection. The lizard and the gazelle will witness your prophethood."

(25) وَالشَّجَرُ والقَمَرُ وَالذِئبُ يَنطِقونَ بِنُبوَّتِكَ عَن قَريبٍ

(25) Wa 'sh-shajaru wa 'l-qamaru wa 'dh-dhi'bu yanṭiqūna bi-nubuwwatika 'an qarīb.

"And the trees, the moon and the wolves will soon pronounce your prophethood."

(26) وَمَرْكَبُكَ البُراقُ إلى جَمالِكَ مُشتَاقٌ

(26) Wa markabuka 'l-burāq ila jamālika mushtāq.

"And the Burāq which will soon become your mount, longs to see your beauty."

(27) وَجِبريلُ شَاوُوشُ مَملَكَتِكَ قَد أَعلنَ بِذِكرِكَ فِي الآفَاقِ

(27) Wa Jibrīlu shāwūshu mamlakatika qad 'a'lana bi-dhikrika fī 'l-'āfāq.

"And Gabriel, as the minister of your kingdom, has declared (your appearance) and has spoken of you across all horizons."

(28) وَالقَمَرُ مَأمُورٌ لَكَ بِالاِنشِقاقِ

(28) Wa 'l-qamaru ma'mūrun laka bi 'l-inshiqāq.

"And the moon as well has been ordered to split for you."

اللهُمَّ صَلِّ وَسَلِّمْ وَبَارِكْ عَلَيْهِ وَعلَىْ آلِه
Allahumma ṣalli wa sallim wa bārik 'alāyh

(29)وَ كُلُّ مَن فِي الكَونِ مُتشَوِّقٌ لِظُهورِكَ، وَمُنتَظِرٌ لِإشْراقِ نُورِكَ

(29) Wa kullu man fī 'l-kawni mutashawwiqun li-ẓuhūrika, wa muntaẓirun li-ishrāqi nūrik.

Every being in the cosmos is longing for your appearance. They are waiting to see your radiant light.

(30) فَبَينَمَا الحَبيبُ صَلَّى اللهُ عَليهِ وَسَلَّمَ مُنصِتٌ لِسَمَاعِ تِلكَ الأَشبَاحِ،
وَوَجْهُهُ مُتَهَلِّلٌ كَنُورِ الصَبَاحِ

(30) Fa baynamā 'l-ḥabību ﷺ munṣitun lisamā'i tilka 'l-ashbaḥ, wa wajhuhu mutahallilun ka-nūri 'ṣ-ṣabāḥ.

While the Beloved ﷺ was quietly listening to their voices, his smiling face was beaming like the morning light.

(31) إِذْ أَقْبَلَتْ حَلِيمَةُ مُعلِنَةً بِالصِّياحِ تَقُولُ: وَاغرِيبَاهُ. فَقالَتِ المَلآئِكَةُ: مَا أَنْتَ يَا مُحَمَّدُ بِغَرِيبٌ، بَلْ أَنْتَ مِن اللهِ قَرِيبٌ، وَأَنتَ لَهُ صَفِيٌّ وَحَبِيبٌ

(31) Idh aqbalat Ḥalīmatu mu'linatan bi 'ṣ-ṣiyāḥ taqūlu: wā gahrībāh! Fa-qālati 'l-malā'ikah: mā anta yā Muḥammad bi-gharīb, bal anta min 'a-Llāhi qarīb wa 'anta lahu ṣafiyyun wa ḥabīb.

Then came Ḥalīmah declaring, crying out, saying, "Pity this strange boy." Then the angels said, "O Muḥammad, you are not strange, but you are close to Allah and you are Allah's best friend and the one loved by Him."

(32) قَالتْ حَلِيمَةُ: وَاوَحِيدَاهُ. فَقَالَتِ المَلآئِكَةُ: يَا مُحَمَّدُ، مَا أَنت بِوَحِيد، بَلْ أَنتَ صَاحِبُ التَّأْيِيدِ، وَأَنِيسُكَ الحَمِيدُ المَجِيدُ! وَإِخْوَانُكَ، إِخوَانُكَ مِنَ المَلآئِكَةِ وَأَهلِ التوحِيدِ

(32) Qālat Ḥalīmatu: wā waḥīdah! Fa-qālati 'l-malā'ikah: yā Muḥammad mā anta bi-waḥīd bal anta ṣāḥibu 't-ta'yīd wa anīsuka 'l-Ḥamīdu 'l-Majīd wa ikhwānuka mina 'l-malā'ikati wa 'ahli 't-tawḥīd.

Again Ḥalīmah said, "Pity, this lonely boy." The angels said, "You are not alone, O Muḥammad! Rather you are the one full of support. Your companion is the Glorious, the Praiseworthy; your friends are the angels and those who believe in the Oneness of Allah."

(33) فَقَالَتْ حَلِيمَةُ: وَايَتِيمَاهُ. فَقَالَتِ المَلآئِكَةُ: للهِ دَرُّكَ مِن يَتِيمٍ، فَإِنَّ قَدرَكَ عِندَ اللهِ عَظِيم

(33) Fa-qālat Ḥalīmah: wā yatīmah! Fa-qālati 'l-malā'ikah: lillāhi darruka min yatīmin, fa inna qadraka 'ind-'aLlāhi 'aẓīm.

Again Ḥalīmah said, "Pity this orphan child!" Then the angels said, "What a glorious praiseworthy one amongst the orphans! Verily you have a tremendous status with Allah."

اللهُمَّ صَلِّ وَسَلِّمْ وَبارِكْ عَلَيْهِ وَعلَىْ آلِه

Allahumma ṣalli wa sallim wa bārik 'alāyh

(34) فَلَمَّا رَأَتْهُ حَلِيمَةُ سَالِمًا مِنَ الأَهْوالِ رَجَعَتْ بِهِ مَسرُورَةً إلى الأَطْلال، ثُمَّ قَصَّتْ خَبَرَهُ عَلَى بَعضِ الكُهَّانِ

(34) Fa-lammā rā'at-hu Ḥalīmatu sāliman mina 'l-'ahwāl raja'at bihi masrūratan ila 'l-'aṭlāli thumma qaṣṣat khabarahu 'alā ba'ḍi 'l-kuhhān.

When Ḥalīmah saw that he ﷺ was safe from danger, she brought him home relieved and happy. Then she narrated the incident to some of the priests.

(35) وَأَعَادَتْ عَلَيهِ مَا تَمَّ مِنْ أَمرِهِ وَمَا كَانَ، فَقَالَ لَهُ الكَاهِنُ: يَا ابْنَ زَمزَمَ وَالمَقَامِ وَالرُكْنِ وَالبَيتِ الحَرامِ، أَفِيْ اليَقْظَةِ رَأَيتَ هَذَا أَمْ فَيْ المَنَامِ

(35) Wa ''ādat 'alāyhi mā tamma min amrihi wa mā kān fa-qāla 'l-kāhinu: yā 'bna zamzama wa 'l-maqām wa 'r-rukni wa 'l-bayti 'l-ḥarām afī 'l-yaqẓati ra'ayta hadhā am fī 'l-manām?

She repeated to the priest what had happened to him ṣalla-Llāhu 'alāyhi wa sallam. So the priest said, "O prince of the Zamzam and the Station of Ibrāhīm, prince of the [Yemeni] Corner and the Sacred House! Were you awake when you experienced these events or were you asleep?"

(36) فَقَالَ وَحُرْمَةِ المَلِكِ العَلَّامِ، شَاهَدتُهُمْ كِفَاحًا لا أَشُكُّ فِي ذَلِكَ وَلاَ أُضَامُ

(36) Faqāla: wa ḥurmati 'l-maliki 'l-'allām shāhadtuhum kifaḥan la ashuku fī dhalika wa lā 'uḍām.

Then the Prophet saw, said, "Rather, with due respect to the King of the Universe, I saw them clearly, there is no doubt in this (experience), and it was not a deception."

(37) فَقَالَ لَهُ الكَاهِنُ: أَبشِرْ أَيُّهَا الغُلامُ، فَأَنتَ صَاحِبُ الأَعلامِ، وَنُبُوَّتُكَ لِلأَنبِيَاءِ قِفْلٌ وَخِتَامٌ، وَعلَيكَ يَنزلُ جِبرِيلُ، وَعَلى بِساطِ القُدسِ يُخَاطِبُكَ الجَلِيلُ، وَمَنْ ذَا الذِيْ يَحْصُرُ مَا حَويتَ مِنَ التَفضِيلِ، وَعَنْ بَعضِ وَصفِ مَعنَاكَ يَقصُرُ لِسَانُ المَادِحِ المُطِيلِ

(37) Fa-qāla lahu 'l-kāhinu: abshir ayyuhā 'l-ghulām fa anta ṣaḥibu 'l-a'lāmi wa nubuwwatuka li 'l-anbiyā'ī quflun wa khitām, 'alayka yanzilu Jibrīlu wa 'alā bisāṭi 'l-qudsi yukhāṭibuka 'l-Jalīl wa man dha 'l-ladhī yaḥṣuru mā ḥawayta mina 't-tafḍīl, wa 'an ba'ḍi waṣfi ma'nāka yaqṣuru lisānu 'l-mādihi 'l-muṭīl.

Then said the priests, "O child! Rejoice because you are the "Leader of the Nations". Your Prophethood is the key and seal. The angel Gabriel will descend upon you. And upon the carpet of holiness, Allah, the Lofty, will address you. Who can circumscribe what excellences are in your possession? The praiser's tongue is incapable of describing even a fraction of your esteemed qualities."

اللهُمَّ صَلِّ وَسَلِّمْ وَبارِكْ عَلَيْهِ وَعلَىْ آلِه ***Allaḥumma ṣalli wa sallim wa bārik ʿalāyh wa ʿala ʿālihi***

(38) وَكَانَ صَلَّىْ اللهُ عليهِ وَسَلَّمَ أَحسَنَ النَاسِ خَلقاً وَخُلُقاً، وَأَهْدَاهُمْ إِلَىْ الحَقِّ طُرُقاً، وَكَانَ خُلُقُهُ القُرْآنَ

(38) Wa kāna ﷺ aḥsana 'n-nāsi khalqan wa khuluqan, wa ahdāhum ila 'l-ḥaqqi ṭuruqan wa kāna khuluquhu 'l-Qur'ān.

Let it be known that Allāh's Messenger ﷺ was the best of mankind, physically and in character, the most righteous in his guidance to the path of truth, His Character was the Qur'an.

(39) وَشِيمَتُهُ الغُفرَانَ، يَنصَحُ لِلإِنْسَانِ، وَيَفسَحُ فِيْ الإِحْسَانِ، وَيَعفُوَ عَنِ الذَنبِ إِنْ كَانَ فِيْ حَقِّهِ وَسَبَبِهِ

(39) Wa shīmatuhu 'l-ghufran, yanṣaḥu li 'l-insān wa yafsaḥu fi 'l-iḥsān, wa yaʿfū ʿani 'dh-dhanbi in kāna fī ḥaqqihi wa sababih.

Pardon was his special trait, he gives advice to man, his excellence was vast, he forgives the sins of others when they transgress against his rights;

(40) فَإِذَا ضُيِّعَ حَقُّ اللهِ لَمْ يَقُمْ أَحَدٌ لِغَضَبِهِ، مَنْ رَآهُ بَدِيهَةً هَابَهُ، وَإِذَا دَعَاهُ المِسكِينُ أَجَابَهُ

(40) Fa idhā ḍuyyiʿa ḥaqqu 'Llāhi lam yaqum aḥadun li-ghaḍabih, man ra'āhu badīhatan hābah, wa idhā daʿāhu 'l-miskīnu ajābah.

But when the rights of Allah were transgressed against, no one could stand before his anger. Whoever saw him, respected him by intuition. When the poor called upon him, he always responded.

(41) يَقُولُ الحَقَّ وَلَوْ كَانَ مُرًّا، وَلاَ يُضْمِرُ لِمُسلِمٍ غِشًّا وَلا ضُرًّا

(41) Yaqūlu 'l-haqqa wa law kāna murran, wa lā yuḍmiru li-muslimin ghishan wa lā ḍurran.

The Prophet spoke the truth however bitter it might be and he never bid in his heart any harm or malice towards Muslims.

(42) مَنْ نَظَرَ فِيْ وَجْهِهِ عَلِمَ أَنَّهُ لَيسَ بِوَجْهِ كَذَّابٍ، وَكَانَ صَلَّى اللهُ عَليهِ وَسَلَّمَ لَيسَ بِغَمَّازٍ وَلا عَيَّابٍ

(42) Man naẓara fī wajhihi ʿalima annahu laysa bi-wajhi kadhdhābin wa kāna ﷺ laysa bi-ghammāzin wa lā ʿayyābin.

Whoever looked at his face recognized that his was not the face of a liar. Verily, God's Messenger ﷺ never criticized or shamed others.

(43) إذا سُرَّ كَأَنَّ وَجهَهُ قِطعَةُ قَمرٍ، وَإذَا كَلَّمَ النَّاسَ، فَكَأنَمَا يَجْنُونَ مِنْ كَلامهِ أَحلَىْ ثَمرٍ

(43) Idhā surra fa-ka'anna wajhahu qiṭ'atu qamarin, wa idhā kallama 'n-nāsa fa-ka-annamā yajnūna min kalāmihi 'aḥlā thamar.

Whenever the Prophet was happy, his face beamed like the crescent. When he spoke, his words appeared as if the people were picking sweet fruits from his mouth.

(44) وَإذَا تَبَسَّمَ تَبسَّمَ عَنْ مِثلِ حَبِّ الغَمَامِ، وَإذَا تَكلَّمَ فكَأَنَّ الدُّرَّ يَسقُطُ مِن ذَلِكَ الكَلامِ، وَإذَا تَحَدَثَ فَكَأَنَّ المِسكَ يَخرُجُ مِن فِيهِ،

(44) Wa idhā tabassama tabbassama 'an mithli ḥabbi 'l-ghamām, wa idhā takallama fa-ka'anna 'ddurrā yasqutu min dhālika 'l-kalām, wa idhā taḥaddatha fa-ka-'anna 'l-miska yakhruju min fīh.

When he smiled, the whiteness of his teeth appeared like patches of clouds. Whenever he spoke, it was as if pearls were falling from his mouth not words. Whenever he spoke about something, it was like musk emanating from his mouth.

(45) وَإذَا مَرَّ بِطَرِيقٍ عُرِفَ مِنْ طِيبِهِ أَنَّهُ قَد مَرَّ فِيهِ

(45) Wa idhā marra biṭarīqin 'urifa min ṭībihi annahu qad marra fīhī.

Whenever he passed by certain places, he left a pleasant aroma and one knew he had passed by from the sweet fragrance he left behind,

(46) وَإذَا جَلَسَ فِي مَجلِسٍ بَقِيَ طِيبُهُ فِيهِ أَيَاماً وانْ تَغيَّبَ، ويُوجَدُ مِنْهُ أَحسَنُ طِيبٍ، وَإنْ لَمْ يَكُنْ قَدْ تَطيَّبَ

(46) Wa idhā jalasa fī majlisin baqīya ṭībuhu fīhi ayyāman wa 'in taghayyab, wa yujadu minhu aḥsanu ṭībin wa in lam yakun qad taṭayyab.

Whenever he sat in a congregation his scent lingered for a few days. The best fragrance emanated from him, though he had not used perfume.

(47) وَإذَا مَشَىْ بَينَ أَصحَابِهِ فَكَأَنَّهُ القَمَرُ بينَ النُجُومِ الزُّهَرِ

(47) Wa idhā mashā bayna aṣḥābihi fa-ka'annahu 'l-qamaru banyan- 'nujūmi 'z-zuhar.

If he walked amongst his companions, it was as if the moon was surrounded by sparkling stars.

(48) وَإذَا أَقبَلَ لَيْلاً فَكَأَنَّ النَّاسَ مِنْ نُورِهِ فِيْ أَوَانِ الظُّهرِ

(48) Wa idhā aqbal laylan fa-ka-anna 'n-nāsa min nūrihi fī awāni 'ẓ-ẓuhr.
Whenever he approached a place at night, his light appeared to the people felt as if it were noon time.

(49) وَكَانَ صَلَّى اللهُ عَليهِ وَسَلَّمَ أَجوَدَ بِالخَيرِ مِنَ الريحِ المُرسَلَةِ، وَكَانَ يُرفِقُ باليَتيمِ وَالأَرمَلَةِ

(49) Wa kāna ﷺ ajwada bi 'l-khayri mina 'r-rīḥi 'l-mursalah, wa kāna yarfuqu bi 'l-yatīmi wa 'l-armalah.
And God's Messenger ﷺ was very generous with his wealth more than the winds which carry rain clouds, and he treated with kindness the orphans and widows.

(50) وَقَالَ بَعضُ وَاصِفِيهِ مَا رَأَيْتُ مِنْ ذِيْ لُمَّةٍ سَودَاءِ فِي حُلَّةٍ حَمرَاءَ، أَحسَنَ مِنْ رَسُولِ اللهِ صَلَّى اللهُ عَليهِ وَسَلَّمَ

(50) Wa qāla baʿḍu wāṣifīhi mā ra'aytu dhi lummatin sawdā' fī ḥullatin ḥamrā', aḥsana min rasūlilLāh ﷺ.
Some companions of his describers said of him, "I have not seen anyone more attractive with black turban and red cloak than he, Allāh's Messenger ﷺ."

اللهُمَّ صَلِّ وَسَلِّمْ وَبارِكْ عَلَيْهِ وَعلَىْ آلِه
Allaḥumma ṣalli wa sallim wa bārik ʿalāyh Wa ʿala 'ālih

(51) وَقِيلَ لِبَعضِهِمْ: كَأَنَّ وَجهَهُ القَمَرْ، فَقَالَ: بَلْ أَضْوَأُ مِنَ القَمَرِ، إِذَا لَمْ يَحُلْ دُونَهُ الغَمَامُ. قَدْ غَشِيَهُ الجَلالُ وَانْتَهَى إِلَيْهِ الكَمَالُ

(51) Wa qīla li-baʿḍihim: ka-anna wajhahu 'l-qamar, fa-qāla: bal aḍwa'u mina 'l-qamar idhā lam yaḥul dūnahu 'l-ghamāmu qad ghashiyahu 'l-jalāl w 'antahā ilayhi 'l-kamāl.
It was said to some people (who saw him), "His face was like the full moon" they said, "his face was even brighter than the moon when it had no cloud covering it." He was fully dressed with beauty, and perfection reached its fullness with him.

(52) قَالَ بَعضُ وَاصِفيهِ: مَا رَأَيْتُ قَبْلَهُ وَلاَ بَعدَهُ مِثلَهُ

(52) Qāla baʿḍu waṣifīhi: mā ra'aitu qablahu wa lā baʿdahu mithlah.
One of those who described him said, "I have never seen anyone like him, before him or after him."

(53) فَيَعجَزُ لِسَانُ البَلِيغِ إِذَا أَرَادَ أَنْ يُحْصِيَ فَضْلَهُ

(53) Fa ya'jazu lisānu 'l-balīghi idhā arāda an yuḥsī faḍlah.
Even the most eloquent tongue fails to describe his excellence.

(54) فَسُبْحَانَ مَنْ خَصَّهُ صَلَّى اللهُ عَليهِ وَسَلَّمَ بِالمَحَلِّ الأَسْنَى، وَأَسْرَى بِهِ إِلَى قَابِ قَوسَينِ أَوْ أَدْنَى

(54) Fa-subḥāna man khaṣṣahu ṣallal-Lahu 'alayhi wa sallam bi 'l-maḥalli 'l-asnā, wa asrā bihi ila qābi qawsayni aw adnā.
Glorified be the One Who exclusively placed him ṣalla-Llāhu 'alāyhi wa sallam in an elevated place, and who caused him ṣalla-Llāhu 'alāyhi wa sallam to travel the night journey *"the distance of two bow's length or nearer still."*

(55) وَأَيَّدَهُ بِالْمُعْجِزَاتِ الَّتِي لاَ تُحْصَى

(55) Wa ayyadahu bi 'l-mu'jizāti 'l-latī lā tuḥṣā,
And supported him with uncountable miracles,

(56) وَأَوْفَاهُ مِنْ خِصَالِ الكَمَالِ مَا يَجِلُّ أَنْ يُسْتَقْصَى، وَأَعْطَاهُ خَمْسَةٌ لَمْ يُعْطِهِنَّ أَحَداً قَبلَهُ

(56) Wa awfāhu min khiṣāli 'l-kamāl ma yajillu an yustaqṣā, wa 'a'ṭāhu khamsatun lam yu'ṭihinna aḥadan qablah.
And equipped him with perfect qualities that are difficult to fully describe and gave him five favors that were never given to anyone before him.

(57) وَآتَاهُ جَوَامِعَ الكَلِمِ، فَلَمْ يُدرِكْ أَحَدٌ فَضْلَهُ

(57) Wa 'ātāhu jawāmi'a 'l-kalimi fa-lam yudrik 'aḥadun faḍlah,
And he granted him the full spectrum of knowledge; In short, no one could achieve his special status.

(58) وَكَانَ لَهُ فِيْ كُلِّ مَقَامٍ مَقَالٌ، وَلِكُلِّ كَمَالٍ مِنهُ كَمَالٌ

(58) Wa kān lahu fī kulli maqāmin maqāl, wa li-kulli kamālin minhu kamāl.
In every station he had a seat, and of every perfection he had perfection.

(59) لاَ يَحُورُ فِيْ سُؤَالٍ وَلاَ جَوَابٍ، وَلاَ يَجُولُ لِسَانُهُ إِلاَّ فِيْ صَوَابٍ

(59) lā yaḥūru fī sū'ālin wa lā jawāb, wa lā yajūlu lisānuhu illa fī ṣawāb.
He never puzzled at any question or response, and his tongue never uttered but the truth.

اللهُمَّ صَلِّ وَسَلِّمْ وَبَارِكْ عَلَيْهِ وَعَلَىْ آلِه

Allahumma ṣalli wa sallim wa bārik 'alāyh

Wa 'ala 'ālih

(60) وَمَا عَسَىٰ أَنْ يُقَالَ فِي مَنْ وَصَفَهُ القُرْآنْ، وَأَعْرَبَ عَنْ فَضَائِلِهِ التَوْرَاةُ
وَالإِنجِيلُ وَالزَبُورُ والفُرقَانُ

(60) Wa mā 'asā an yuqālu fī man waṣafahu 'l-Qur'ān, wa ā'araba 'an faḍā'ilihi 't-Tawrātu wa 'l-Injīlu wa 'z-Zabūru 'l-Furqān.

What more can be said of the person who was described in the Qur'ān, and whose qualities were made known in the Torah, Gospel, Book of Psalms and the Criterion?

(61) وَجَمَعَ اللهُ لَهُ بَينَ رُؤْيَتِهِ وَكَلامِهِ، وَقَرَنَ إِسْمَهُ مَعَ إِسْمِهِ تَنْبِيهاً عَلَىٰ عُلُوِّ مَقَامِهِ

(61) Wa jama'a Allāhu lahu bayna ru'yatihi wa kalāmihi, wa qaran ismahu ma'a ismihi tanbihan 'alā 'uluwwi maqāmih.

And Allah made his vision and his word to be one and the same. Allah honored him by associating his name with His Name, in order to show and prove his high station,

(62) وَجَعَلَهُ رَحمَةً لِلْعَالَمِينَ وَنُوراً، وَمَلأَ بِمَوْلِدِهِ القُلُوبَ سُرُوراً

(62) Wa ja'alahu raḥmatan li 'l-'ālamina wa nūran, wa mal'a bi-mawlidihi 'l-qulūba surūra.

And He ﷻ made him to be a mercy for all the worlds, and filled all hearts with happiness because of his birth.

اللهُمَّ صَلِّ وَسَلِّمْ وَبَارِكْ عَلَيْهِ وَعلَىٰ آلِه
Allaḥumma ṣalli wa sallim wa bārik 'alāyh
Wa 'ala 'ālih

13 - Yā Nabī Salām ʿAlayka

يَا نَبِي سَلامْ عَلَيكَ	يَا رَسُولْ سَلامْ عَلَيكَ
يَا حَبِيبْ سَلامْ عَلَيكَ	صَلَوَاتُ اللهِ عَلَيكَ
Yā Nabī salām ʿalayka	*Yā Rasūl salām ʿalayka*
Yā Ḥabīb salām ʿalayka	*Ṣalawātullāh ʿalayka*

(1) أَشرَقَ الكَونُ اِبتِهَاجًا   بِوُجُودِ المُصْطَفَىْ أَحْمَدْ

Ashraqa ʾl-kawnu ʾbtihājan   Bi wujūdi ʾl-musṭaf ʾAḥmad

The universe shined with delight rejoicing in the existence of Chosen One, Ahmad.

(2) وَلأَهلِ الكَونِ أُنسٌ   وَسُرُورٌ قَدْ تَجَدَّدْ

Wa li ʾahli ʾl-kawni unsun   Wa sururun qad tajaddad

And the inhabitants of the universe found intimacy, And a renewed happiness

(3) فَاطرَبُوا يَا اهْلَ المَثَانِي   فَهَزَارُ اليُمْنِ غَرَّدْ

Faṭrabū yā ʾahla ʾl-mathānī   Fa hazāru ʾl-yumni gharrad

(The nightingale sang:) 'Be delighted, O settler of the two places (heavens and earth) with this good fortune."

(4) وَاستَضِيئُوا بِجَمَالٍ   فَاقَ فِيْ الحُسْنِ تَفَرَّدْ

Wa ʾstaḍīʾū bi jamālin   Fāqa fīl-ḥusni tafarrad

And seek the light from such a beauty, That is exceedingly superior and unique.

(5) وَلَنَا البُشرَىْ بِسَعْدٍ   مُسْتَمِرٍ لَيْسَ يَنفَدْ

Wa lanā ʾl-bushrā bi saʿdin   Mustamirrin laysa yanfad

We received the good news, With continuous happiness never ending.

(6) حَيثُ أُوتِينَا عَطَاءً   جَمَعَ الفَخرَ المُؤَبَّدْ

Ḥaythu ʾūtīnā ʿaṭāʾan   Jamaʿa ʾl-fakhra ʾl-muʾabbad

As we were given a gift, That encompassed eternal glory (for this life and the hereafter).

(7) فَلِرَبي كُلُّ حَمدٍ   جَلَّ أَنْ يَحْصُرَهُ العَدْ

Fa li Rabbī kullu ḥamdin   Jalla an yaḥṣurahu 'l-ʿad
For my Lord all praises and, Thanks that are countless in number.

(8) إِذْ حَبَانَا بِوُجُودِ   المُصْطَفَىْ الهَادِيْ مُحَمَّدْ

Idh ḥabānā bi wujūdi   'l-Muṣṭafā 'l-hādī Muḥammad
Since He bestowed upon us, the presence (birth) of Muḥammad, the Chosen One and the Guide.

اللهُمَّ صَلِّ وَسَلِّمْ وَبَارِكْ عَلَيْهِ وَعلَىْ آلِه

Allāhuma ṣalli wa sallim wa bārik ʿalayhi wa ʿalā ʿālih

14 - Marḥaban Marḥaban

مَرْحَبًا مَرْحَبًا يَا نُوْرَ عَيْنِي

Marḥaban Marḥaban yā nūru ʿaynī

Greetings! Greetings! O the light of my eyes!

مَرْحَبًا مَرْحَبًا جَدَّ الْحُسَيْنِ

Marḥaban Marḥaban jadda ʾl-Ḥūsayni

Greetings! Greetings! grandfather of al-Ḥusayn

(1) مَرْحَبًا يَا رَسُوْلَ اللهِ أَهْلاً مَرْحَبًا بِكَ إِنَّا بِكَ نُسْعَدْ

Marḥaban Yā RasūlaLlāhi ʾahlan Marḥaban bika innā bika nusʿad

Greetings! Prophet of Allāh, Greetings! Welcome, for verily with you is our happiness

(2) مَرْحَبًا.. وَبِجَاهِهْ يَا إِلَهِيْ مَرْحَبًا.. جُدْ وَبَلِّغْ كُلَّ مَقْصَدْ

Marḥaban wa bi jāhih yā ilāhī Marḥaban jud wa balligh kulla maqṣad

Greetings! For the sake of his high honored rank, O our Lord, Welcome, give generously and fulfill all our intentions

(3) مَرْحَبًا.. وَاهْدِنَا نَهْجَ سَبِيْلِه مَرْحَبًا.. كَيْ بِهِ نُسْعَدْ وَنُرْشَدْ

Marḥaban wa ʾhdinā nahja sabīlih Marḥaban kay bihi nusʿad wa nurshad

Greetings, Guide us with his methods and directions, Welcome, so that we receive happiness and guidance.

رَبِّ فَاغْفِرْ لِيْ ذُنُوبِيْ يَا الله
Rabba f'aghfir lī dhunūbī yā Allāh
O my Lord, forgive me, my sins, O Allāh
بِبَرْكَةِ الْهَادِيْ مُحَمَّدْ يَا الله
Bi-barakati 'l-hādī Muḥammad yā Allāh
With the blessings of the guide Muḥammad, O Allāh

(1) رَبِّ بَلِّغْنَا بِجَاهِهْ يا الله فِي جِوَارِه خَيْرَ مَقْعَدْ يا الله

Rabbī ballighnā bi jāhih ya Allāh fī jiwārihi khayra maqʿad ya Allāh

O my Lord, let us reach (our goal) for the sake of his high rank (with You) In his proximity is the best place to stay, O Allāh

(2) وَصَلاَةُ اللهِ تَغْشَى يا الله أَشْرَفَ الرُّسْلِ مُحَمَّدْ يا الله

wa ṣalātullāhi tagshā ya Allāh ashrafar-rusli Muḥammad ya Allāh

And may Allāh's blessings shower, O Allah The Noblest of all the Messengers, Muḥammad O Allah.

(3) وَسَلامٌ مُسْتَمِرٌّ يا الله كُلَّ حِيْنٍ يَتَجَدَّدْ يا الله

wa salāmun mustamirrun ya Allāh kulla ḥīnin yatajaddad ya Allāh.

Peace be upon him without end o Allah, Greetings, renewed with every moment o Allah.

اللهُمَّ صَلِّ وَسَلِّمْ وَبَارِكْ عَلَيْهِ وَعَلَىٰ آلِه
Allāhuma ṣalli wa sallim wa bārik ʿalayhi wa ʿalā ālih

15 - Ṭalaʿa ʼl-Badru ʿAlaynā

طَلَعَ البَدْرُ عَلَينَا مِنْ ثَنِيَاتِ الوَدَاعِ

Ṭalaʿa ʼl-badru ʿalaynā Min thaniyyāti ʼl-wadāʿa

The full moon rose above us

From the valley of Wadāʿa

وَجَبَ الشُكرُ عَلَينَا مَا دَعَا للهِ دَاعِ

Wajabash-shukru ʿalaynā Mā daʿā li ʼl-Lāhi dāʿ

Gratitude is our obligation

as long as any caller calls to Allāh 2x

(1) أَيُّهَا المَبْعُوثُ فِينَا جِئتَ بِالأَمرِ المُطَاعِ

Ayyuha ʼl-mabʿūthu fīnā Jiʼta bi ʼl-amri ʼl-muṭāʿa

O you who were sent among us, you came with the orders to be obeyed

(2) كُنْ شَفِيعًا يَا حَبِيبِي يَومَ حَشرٍ وَاجْتِمَاعِ

Kun shafīʿan yā ḥabībī Yawma ḥashrin wa ʼjtimāʿ

Be our intercessor O our Beloved, On the Day of collection and gathering

(3) رَبَّنَا صَلِّ عَلَى مَنْ حَلَّ فِي خَيرِ البِقَاعِ

Rabbanā ṣalli ʿalā man Ḥalla fī khayru ʼl-biqāʿ

O our Lord send your blessings on the one, Who appeared in the best of all places,

(4) أَنتَ غَوثُنَا جَمِيعًا يَا مُجَمَّلَ الطِبَاعِ

Anta ghawthunā jamīʿan Yā mujammala ʼṭ-ṭibāʿ

You are the savior of us all, O you with the perfected character

(5) وَلَبِسنَا ثَوبَ عِزٍّ بَعدَ تَلفِيقِ الرِقَاعِ

Wa labisnā thawba ʿizzin Baʿda talfiqi ʼrriqāʿ

We were adorned with the robe of honor, after wearing patches and tatters

(6) أَسبِلِ السِّترَ عَلَينَا يَا مُجِيبًا كُلَّ دَاعِي

Asbili ʼs-sitra ʿalaynā Yā mujīban kulla dāʿ

Cover us up our shortcomings, O Answerer of all requests

(7) وَصَلاَةُ اللهِ عَلَى أَحمَدْ   عَدَّ تَحرِيرِ الرِّقَاعِ

Wa ṣalātuLlāh ʿalā ʿAḥmad   ʿAdda taḥrīri ʿrriqāʿ

And Allāh's blessing be upon Aḥmad, on the numbers of the freed lands

(8) وكَذَا آلٍ وصَحبٍ   مَا سَعَىْ للهِ سَاعِ

Wa kadhā ʿālin wa ṣaḥbin   Mā saʿa li ʿl-Lāhi sāʿ

And likewise upon the Family and the Companions, as long as the striving is for Allāh.

اللهُمَّ صَلِّ وَسَلِّمْ وَبَارِكْ عَلَيْهِ وَعلَىْ آلِه
Allāhuma ṣalli wa sallim wa bārik ʿalayhi wa ʿalā ālih

16 - Ṭālamā Ashkū Gharāmī

طَالَمَا أَشكُو غَرَامِي يَا نُورَ الوجُود

Ṭālamā ashkū gharāmī Yā nūral wujūd

I continue to comlain of my love for you, O Light of all Existence!

وَ أُنادِي يَاتِهَامِي يَامَعْدِنَ الجُود

Wa unādī yā tihāmī Yā ma'dina 'l-jūd

And I call upon the one fromTihama, O mine of generosity

(1) مُنيَتِي أقْصَى مَرَامِي أحْظَى بِالشُّهُود

Munyatī aqṣā marāmī ***Aḥẓā bi 'sh-shuhūd***

My hope, the limit of my prospects, is to attain witnessing

(2) وَأرَى بَابَ السَّلَامِ يَا زَكِي الجُدود

Wa arā bāba 's-salāmi ***Yā zakīl-judūd***

And to see the Gate of Peace, O descendant of pure fathers

(3) يَا طِرَازَ الكَوْنِ إنِّي عَاشِق مُستَهَام

Yā ṭirāza 'l-kawni innī ***'āshiq mustahām***

O archetype of all creation, truly I am a lover, forlorn

(4) مُغرَمٌ وَالمَدحُ فَنِّي يَابدرَ التَمَام

Mughramun wa 'l-madḥu fannī

Yā badra't-tamām

Enamored and praise is my art, O full moon of perfection

(5) إصرِفِ الإعْرَاضَ عَنِّي أضنَانِي الغَرَام

Iṣrifi 'l-'i'rāḍa 'annī ***Aḍnānīl-gharām***

Remove your aversion from me, Your love has exhausted me,

(6) فِيكَ قَد أحسَنتُ ظَنِّي يَا سَامِي العُهُود

Fīka qad aḥsantu ẓannī ***Yā sami'-l-'uhūd***

In you I have best expectation, O fulfiller of promises

(7) يَا سِرَاجَ الأَنبِيَاءِ يَا عَالِي الجَنَاب

Yā sirāja 'l-anbiyā'i ***Yā 'Ālī 'l-janāb***

O Sun of the prophets, O possessor of highest honor

(8) يَا إِمَامَ الأَتقِيَاءِ إِنّ قَلْبِي ذَاب

Yā 'imāma 'l-atqiyā'i	***Inna qalbī dhāb***
O leader of the God-wary,	Truly my Heart is melting,

(9) وَ عَلَيك اللّهُ صَلَّى رَبي ذُو الجَلَال

Wa 'alayka-Allāhu ṣallā	***Rabbī Dhu 'l-jalāl***
And upon You Allāh sends blessings,	My Lord of Majesty

(10) يَكفِي يَا نُورَ الأَهِلَّة إِنّ هَجرِي طَال

Yakfī yā nūra 'l-ahilla	***Inna hajrī ṭāl***
Enough, O light of the crescents,	You have abandoned me for too long.

اللهُمَّ صَلِّ وَسَلِّمْ وَبَارِكْ عَلَيْهِ وَعلَىْ آلِه

Allāhuma ṣalli wa sallim wa bārik 'alayhi wa 'alā ālih

17 - Ṣall-Allāhu ʿalā Muḥammad

صَلَّى اللهُ عَلَى مُحَمَّدْ

Ṣall-Allāhu ʿalā Muḥammad

صَلَّى اللهُ عَلَيهِ وَسَلَّمْ

Ṣall-Allāhu ʿalayhi wa sallam 2x

(1) رَبِّ وَاجْعَلْ مُجتَمَعنَا غَايَتهُ حُسنُ الخِتَامِ

Rabbī wajʿal mujtamaʿnā ***Ghāyatu ḥusnu ʾl-khitāmi***

O my Lord, make our gathering's Purpose a good ending

(2) وَاعْطِنَا مَا قَدْ سَأَلْنَا مِنْ عَطَايَاكَ الْجِسَامِ

Wa āʿaṭinā mā qad saʾalnā ***Min ʿaṭāyāka ʾl-jisāmi***

And grant us what we are asking, from your great favors

(3) وَاكرِمِ الأَروَاحَ مِنَّا بِلِقَى خَيرِ الأَنَامِ

W'akrimi ʾl-ʾarwāḥa minnā ***Bi liqā khayri ʾl-anāmi***

And bless the souls among us, with A meeting with the Best of Created beings,

(4) وَابْلِغِ الْمُختَارَ عَنَّا مِنْ صَلاَةٍ وَسَلاَمِ

W'ablighi ʾl-mukhtāra ʿannā ***Min ṣalātin wa salāmi***

And convey to the Chosen One, from us, Blessings and greetings of peace,

(5) يَا اللهُ يَا مُحَمَّدْ يَا أَبَا بَكرْ يَا صِدِّيقْ

Yā Allāhu Yā Muḥammad ***Yā Abā Bakr Aṣ-Ṣiddīq***

O Allāh, O Muḥammad, O Abū Bakr Aṣ-Ṣiddīq

(6) يَا عُمَرْ عُثمَانْ يَا عَلِي فَاطِمَةْ بِنتَ رَسُولِ

Yā ʿUmar ʿUthmān Yā ʿAlī ***Fāṭimah binta Rasūli.***

O ʿUmar, ʿUthmān, O ʿAlī, Fāṭimah daughter of the Prophet

اللهُمَّ صَلِّ وَسَلِّمْ وَبَارِكْ عَلَيْهِ وَعلَىْ آلِه

Allāhuma ṣalli wa sallim wa bārik ʿalayhi wa ʿalā ʿālih

18- Yā Arḥama ʼr-Rāḥimīn

يَاأَرحمَ الرّاحِمِين يَاأَرحمَ الرّاحِمِين

Yā Arḥama ʼr-Rāḥimīn 3x

O Most Merciful of the merciful ones

يَاأَرحمَ الرّاحِمِين فَرِّج عَلَى المُسلِمِين

Farrij ʿalā ʼl-muslimīn

Send relief on to the Muslims

(1) يَاأَرحمَ الرّاحِمِين يَاأَرحمَ الرّاحِمِين

Yā Arḥamar-Rāḥimīn 3x

O Most Merciful of the merciful ones

(2) يَاأَرحمَ الرّاحِمِين فَرِّج عَلَى المُسلِمِين

Yā Arḥamar-Rāḥimīn ***Farrij ʿalā ʼl-muslimīn***

Send salvation to the Muslims

(3) يَارَبَنّا يَاكَرِيم يَارَبَنّا يَارَحِيم

Yā Rabbanā Yā Karīm, ***Yā Rabbanā Yā Raḥīm***

O our generous Lord, O our Merciful Lord!

(4) أَنتَ الجَوَادُ الحَلِيم و أَنتَ نِعمَ المُعِينَ

Anta ʼl-Jawādu ʼl-Ḥalīm, ***Wa Anta niʿma ʼl-muʿīn***

You are the One who gives and the One with forbearance, and the best One who assists

(5) وَ مَا لَنَا رَبّنَا سِوَاكَ يَا حَسبُنَا

Wa mā lanā Rabbanā, ***Siwāka yā ḥasbuna***

Our Lord we have none to rely on but You

(6) يَاذَاالعُلَا وَالغِنَا وَ يَا قَوِي يَا مَتِين

Yā Dha ʼl-ʿulā wa ʼl-Ghinā, ***wa Yā Qawī Yā Matīn***

O Most High and Self-sufficient One, O Strong and Firm One!

(7) وَ لَيسَ نَرجُو سِوَاك فَادرِك إِلٰهِي دَرَاك

Wa laysa narjū siwāk, ***Fadrik ilāhī darāk***

We seek none but You, so reach us and look after us

(8) قَبلَ الفَنَا وَالهَلَاك   يَعُمُّ دُنيا وَ دِين

Qabla 'l-fanā wa 'l-halāk,   Ya'ummu ' dunyā wa dīn
Before annihilation and destruction cover the material world and religion

(9) بجَاهِ طَهَ الرَّسُول   جُد رَبَّنَا بِالقَبُول

Bi jāhi Ṭāha 'r-rasūl,   Jud Rabbanā bi 'l-Qabūl
For the sake of Ṭāhā the Messenger, grant us the favor of our acceptance

(10) وَهَب لَنَا كُلَّ سُؤل   رَبِّ استَجِب لِي آمِين

Wa hab lanā kulla sūl,   Rabbī 'stajib lī amīn
And grant us everything we asked for, my Lord answer my requests, Amīn

(11) وَ اغفِرْ لي كُلَّ الذُنوب   وَاستُر لي كُلَّ العُيُوب

Wa 'ghfir lī kulla 'dh-dhunūb ,   wa 'stur lī kulla 'uyūb
And forgive for me all my sins, and cover for me all my flaws

(12) وَاكشِف لِي كُلَّ الكُرُوب   وَاكفِ أَذَى المُؤذِين

Wa 'kshif lī kulla 'l-kurūb,   wa 'kfi 'adha 'l-mu'dhīn
And lift from me all difficulty, and fend off from me the harm of those harmful ones

(13) وَ اختِم بِأَحسَن خِتَام   إِذَا دَنَا الإنصِرَام

Wa 'khtim bi aḥsan khitām,   Idhā danā 'l-inṣirām
And seal my end with a good ending, when death approaches

(14) وَ حَانَ حَينُ الحِمَام   وَ زَادَ رَشحُ الجَبِين

Wa ḥāna ḥaynu 'l-ḥimām,   Wa zāda rashḥu 'l-jabīn
And when the time for trials arrive, and the sweat of the brow increases

(15) ثُمَّ الصَلَاة وَالسَّلام   عَلى شَفِيعِ الأَنَام

Thummaṣ-ṣalāt wa 's-salām,   'alā shafī'i 'l-anām
Then praise and blessings upon the intercessor of the masses

(16) وَالآلِ نِعمَ الكِرَام   وَالصَّحبِ وَالتّابِعِين

Wa 'l-'ālī ni'ma 'l-kirām,   wa 'ṣ-ṣaḥbi wa 't-tabi'īn
Along with his most honored family, his companions and followers

19 - Yā Rasūlullāhi Salāmun ʿAlayk

يَا رَسُولُ اللهِ سَلامٌ عَلَيك

Yā Rasūlullāhi salāmun ʿalayk

O Prophet of Allāh, peace be on you!

يَا رَفِيعَ الشَانِ وَالدَّرجِ

Yā Rafīʿi ash-shāni wa ʾd-daraji

O Possessor of the highest station and rank

(1) عَطفَةً يَا جِيرَةَ العَلَمِ　　　يَا أُهَيلَ الجُودِ وَالكَرَمِ

ʿaṭfatan yā jīrata ʾl-ʿalami　Yā uhayla ʾl-jūdi wa ʾl-karami

Have sympathy for us, O distinguished neighbor, you who are giving and generous

(2) نَحنُ جِيرَانٌ بِذَا الحَرَمِ　　　حَرَمُ الإِحسَانِ وَالحَسَنِ

Naḥnu jīrānun bi dha ʾl-ḥarami　Ḥaramu ʾl-iḥsāni wa ʾl-ḥasani

We are your neighbors in the Holy Sanctuary, The sanctuary of excellence and goodness

(3) نَحنُ مِن قَومٍ بِهِ سَكَنُوا　　　وَ بِهِ مِن خَوفِهِم أَمِنُوا

Naḥnu min qawmin bihi sakanū　Wa bihi min khawfihim ʾaminū.

We are from amongst a people who through him reached tranquility, And through him no longer stay in fear

(4) وَ بِآيَاتِ القُرآنِ عُنُوا　　　فَاتَّئِد فِينَا أَخَا الوَهَنِ

Wa bi ʾāyāti ʾl-Qurāni ʿunū　Fa ʾt-taʾid fīnā akhāʾl-wahani

And who busied themselves with the verses of the Qur'an, Within us you will not find weakness and lack of courage

(5) نَعرِفُ البَطحَا وَتَعرِفُنَا　　　وَ الصَّفَا وَالبَيتُ يَألَفُنَا

Naʿrifu ʾl-baṭḥā wa taʿrifunā　Waṣ-ṣafā wa ʾl-baytu yaʾlafunā

We know the desert and it knows us, And Ṣafā and the (Holy) House are familiar with us

(6) وَ لَنَا المَعْلَى وَ خَيْفُ مُنَى　　　فَاعَلَمَّن هذَا وَكُن رَكِنِ

Wa lanāʾl-maʿlā wa khayfu munā　Faʿlaman hādhā wa kun rakini

al-Maʿlā and Khīfu Munābelong us, Know that and be clever

(7) وَ لَنَا خَيْرُ الْأَنَامِ أَبُ وَ عَلِيٌّ الْمُرتَضَى حَسَبُ

Wa lanā khayru 'l-anamī abū Wa 'Aliyyu 'l-murtaḍā ḥasabu

The best of creation is our father, And ʿAlī the Blessed, is from us

(8) وَ إِلَى السِّبطَينِ نَنتَسِبُ نَسَبًا مَافِيهِ مِن دَخَنِ

Wa ilā 's-sibṭayni nantasibu Nasabun mā fīhi min dakhini

And to the two lions (Ḥasan and Ḥusayn) we are related, There is no doubt about our lineage

(9) كَم إِمَامٍ بَعدَهُ خَلَفُوا مِنهُ سَادَاتٌ بِذَا عُرِفُوا

Kam 'Imāmin ba'dahu khālafū Minhu sādātun bidhā 'urifū

How many imams came from their progeny, Amongst them are well known masters

(10) وَ بِهَذَا الوَصفِ قَد وُصِفُوا مِن قَدِيمِ الدَّهرِ وَالزَّمَنِ

Wa bi hādhā 'l-waṣfi qad wuṣifū Min qadīmi 'd-dahri waz-zamani

They were described in this manner, Since olden times and previous eras

(11) مِثلُ زَينِ العَابِدِينَ عَلِي وَابنِهِ البَاقِرِ خَيرِ وَلِي

Mithlu zayni 'l-'ābidīna 'Alī W'abnihi 'l-Bāqiri khayri walī

The like of Zayn al-ʿAbidīna ʿAlī, And his son al-Bāqir who is the best of saints

(12) وَالإِمَامِ الصَّادِقِ الحَفِلِ وَ عَلِيٍ ذِي العُلا اليَقِنِ

Wa 'l-'Imāmi 'ṣ-ṣādiqi 'l-ḥafili Wa 'Alīyyin dhi 'l-'ula 'l-yaqini

And the famous Īmām aṣ-Ṣādiq, And ʿAlī of high station and certainty

(13) فَهُم القَومُ الذِينَ هُدُوا وَ بِفَضلِ اللهِ قَد سُعِدُوا

Fa-humu 'l-qawmu 'lladhīnā hudū Wa bi faḍli 'l-āhī qad su'idū

They are the people who were guided, And with Allāh's favor were happy

(14) وَ لِغَيرِ اللهِ مَا قَصَدُوا وَ مَع القُرآنِ فِي قَرَنِ

Wa li ghayri 'l-Lāhi mā qaṣadū Wa m'a 'l-Qur'āni fī qarani

Their only goal was Allāh, Their friend was the Qur' an

(15) أَهلُ بَيتِ المُصطَفَى الطُّهُرِ هُم أَمَانُ الأَرضِ فَادَّكِرِ

'Ahlu bayti 'l-Muṣṭafā 'ṭ-ṭuhuri Hum amānu 'l-arḍi fad-dakiri

The pure family of the Chosen One, They are the guarantee for this earth's safety so be heedful

(16) شُبِّهُوا بِالأَنجُمِ الزُّهُرِ   مِثلَمَا قَد جَآءَ فِي السُّنَنِ

Shubihū bi 'l-anjumi 'z-zuhuri   Mithlamā qad jā'a fī 's-sunani
They were described as the shining stars, As was related in the traditions

(17) وَ سَفِينٌ لِلنَّجَاةِ إِذَا   خِفتَ مِن طُوفَانِ كُلِّ أَذَى

Wa safīnun li 'n-najāti idhā   Khifta min ṭūfāni kulli adhā
And as a ship of safety, If you were afraid of any flood of harmful things

(18) فَانجُ فِيهَا لا تَكُونَ كَذَا   وَا عتَصِم بِاللهِ وَاستَعِنِ

F 'anjū fīhā lā takūnu kadhā   Wa ʿtaṣim bi 'l-Lāhi wastaʿini
So ride this ship and do not be this way And hold on to Allāh and ask his support,

(19) رَبِّ فَانفَعنَا بِبَرَكَتِهِم   وَاهدِنَا الحُسنَى بِحُرْمَتِهِم

Rabbi f 'anfaʿnā bi barakatihim   Wa 'hdinā 'l-ḥusnā bi ḥurmatihim
My Lord benefit us through their blessings, And guide us to goodness for their sake

(20) وَ أَمِتنَا فِي طَرِيقَتِهِم   وَ مُعَافَاةٍ مِنَ الفِتَنِ

Wa amitnā fī ṭarīqatihim   Wa muʿāfātin mina 'l-fitani
And let us die on their path, And to be safe from confusion

اللهُمَّ صَلِّ وَسَلِّمْ وَبَارِكْ عَلَيْهِ وَعَلَىْ آلِه
Allāhuma ṣalli wa sallim wa bārik ʿalayhi wa ʿalā ālih

20 - Burdah

يَا رَبِّ بِالْمُصطَفَى بَلِّغْ مَقَاصِدَنَا

Yā Rabbi bi 'l-Muṣṭafā balligh maqāsidanā

O my Lord! By means of the Chosen One let us achieve our goals

وَاغفِرِ لَنَا مَا مَضَى يَا وَاسِعَ الكَرَمِ

Wa 'ghfirlanā mā maḍā yā wāsi'al-karami

And forgives us our past (misdeeds), O Possessor of Vast Generosity!

(1) يــا أكرَمَ الخلقِ ما لي مَن ألوذُ بهِ   سِـوَاكَ عِنـدَ حُلولِ الحادِثِ العَمَمِ

Yā akrama 'l-khalqi mā lī man alūdhu bihi Siwāka 'inda ḥulūli 'l-ḥādithi 'l-'amami

Most generous of mankind, I have no one to take refuge in except you At the occurrence of widespread calamity.

(2) ولَن يَضِيقَ رسـولَ اللهِ جاهُكَ بي   إذا الكريمُ تجَلَّى بـاسمِ مُنتَقِمِ

Wa lan yaḍīqa rasūl-Allāhi jāhuka bī Idha 'l-karīmu tajallā bismi munṭaqimi

And O Messenger of Allāh, your exalted status will not diminish, from your intercession for me When The Most Bountiful manifests with the Name of the Avenger.

(3) فَإنَّ مِن جُودِكَ الدُنيا وَضَرَّتَهَا   وَمِن عُلومِكَ عِلمَ اللَـوحِ وَالقَلَمِ

Fa inna min jūdika 'd-dunyā wa ḍārrataha Wa min 'ulūmika 'ilma 'l-lawḥi wa 'l-qalami

For verily amongst your bounties is this world, and the Next.

And of your knowledge is knowledge of the Preserved Tablets, and the Pen.

(4) يا نَفْسُ لا تَقنَطِي مِن زَلَّةٍ عَظُمَتْ   إنَّ الكَبَـائِرَ في الغُفرَانِ كـاللَّمَـمِ

Yā nafsu lā taqnaṭī min zallatin 'aẓumat Inna 'l-kabā'ira fī 'l-ghufrāni ka 'l-lamami

O my self do not despair due to your grave sins.

Truly even the greatest sins when pardoned are minor.

(5) لعَـلَّ رَحمَةَ رَبِّي حينَ يَقسِـمُهَا تَأتِي على حَسَبِ العِصيَان في القِسَمِ

Lʿalla raḥmata Rabbī ḥīna yaqsimuhā Taʾtī ʿalā ḥasabi ʾl-ʿiṣyāni fīl-qisami

Perhaps the mercy of my Lord when distributed,
Will be distributed in proportion to the sins.

(6) يا رَبِّ واجعَلْ رجائِي غيرَ مُنعَكِسٍ لَدَيْـكَ واجعلْ حِسَابِي غيرَ مُنخَرِمِ

Yā Rabbi wʾajʿal rajāʾī ghayra munʿakisin Ladayka wʾajʿal ḥisābi ghayra munkharimi

O my Lord! Make my hopes not rejected by You, And make my reckoning not reveal my deficiencies.

(7) والطُفْ بِعَبدِكَ في الدَّارَينِ إنَّ لَـهُ صَبراً مَتَى تَـدْعُهُ الاَهْـوالُ ينهَزِمِ

Wa ʾl-ṭuf bi ʿabdika fī ʾd-dārayni inna lahu Ṣabran matā tadʿuhu ʾl-ahwālu yanhazimi

Be kind to Your servant in both worlds, for verily his
patience, when called upon by hardships (calamities), runs away.

(8) وائذَنْ لِسُحْبِ صلاةٍ منك دائِمَةٍ عَـلى النبيِّ بِمُنْهَـلٍّ ومُنسَجِمِ

Wa ʾdhan li-suḥbi ṣalātin minka dāʾimatin ʿala ʾn-nabīyi bi-munhalin wa munsajimi

So order clouds of blessings (salutations) from you perpetually.
Upon the Prophet ﷺ abundantly and gently

(9) والآلِ والصَّحبِ ثُمَّ التَّابعِينَ فَهُـمْ أهلُ التُّقى والنَّقى والحِلْمِ والكَـرَمِ

Wa ʾl-ʾālī wa ʾṣ-ṣaḥbi thumma ʾt-tābiʿīna lahum ʾAhlut-tuqā wa ʾn-naqā wa ʾl-ḥilmi wa ʾl-karami

And upon his family his Sahabah, then upon those who follow them.
The people of piety, knowledge, clemency and generosity.

اللهُمَّ صَلِّ وَسَلِّمْ وَبَارِكْ عَلَيْهِ وَعلَىْ آلِه

Allāhuma ṣalli wa sallim wa bārik ʿalayhi wa ʿalā ʾālih

21 – Qul Ya ʿAẓīm

قُلْ يَا عَظِيمْ أَنْتَ الْعَظِيمْ   قَدْ هَمَّنَا هَمٌّ عَظِيمْ

Qul Ya ʿAẓīm'Anta 'lʿAẓīm   Qad Hammanā Hāmmun ʿAẓim

Say: O Tremendous One you are the Tremendous; we have been afflicted with a grave concern

وَكُلُّ هَمٍّ هَمَّنَا   يَهُونُ بِاسْمِكَ يَا عَظِيمْ

Wa kullu hāmmin hammanā   yahūnū bi 'smika ya ʿAẓīm

And every concern we are worried about, becomes easy with the mention of your name oh great one

أَنْتَ الْقَدِيمْ قَدِيمٌ فِي الأَزَلْ   أَنْتَ اللَّطِيفْ لَطِيفٌ لَمْ تَزَلْ

عَنَّا ازِلْ مَا قَدْ نَزَلْ   مِنْ فَادِحِ الْخَطْبِ الشَّدِيدْ

Anta 'l-Qadīm Qadīmun fi ' īl'azal   'l-Laṭīf laṭīfun lam tazal
ʿĀnna azil mā qad nazzal   min fādiḥi 'l-khatbi 'sh-shadīd
You are the ancient, ancient one, you are the subtle subtle still
Remove fom us what has befallen us; of grave and difficult afflictions

حَيٌّ قَدِيمْ قَدِيمٌ وَاجِدُ   بَاقِيْ غَنِيْ غَنِيٌّ مَاجِدُ

عَدْلٌ اِلَهْ اِلَهٌ وَاحِدُ   بَرٌّ رَؤوْفْ رَؤوْفٌ بِالعَبِيْدْ

Ḥayyun qadīm qadīmun wājidū   bāqi ghanī ghaniyyun mājidū

ʿAdlun Ilāh Ilāhun wāḥidū   Barrun ra' ūf ra'ūfun bilʿabīd

Living ancient ancient and generous; immortal rich rich and glorius

Just God one God; good tender tender with the servant

وَلِلْنَّبِيِّ صَلِّ يَا سَلَامْ   مِنَّا صَلَاةٌ مَعْ سَلَامْ

يَوْمُ الْجَزَا اِمْنَحْنَا سَلَامْ   مِمَّا نَخَافُ يَا مَجِيدْ

Wa lil-Nabiy ṣalli ya salām   minna ṣalātun maʿ salām

Yawmu 'ljazā 'mnāḥna salām   mīmma nakhāfu yā majīd

And upon the prophet oh Peace, send praise and greetings; from us send greetings and blessings

Grant us safety on judgment day, from all things which we fear oh Glorious one

وَالآلِ وَالْصَّحْبِ الأُسُودْ   سَادُوا بِهِ بِيضًا وَسُودْ

لا سِيَّمَا مَاحِيْ الْحُشُودْ   سَيفُ الإلَه إبنُ الوَلِيدْ

Wa 'l'āli wa 'ṣ-ṣāḥbi 'l'usūd; sādu bihi bīḍan wa sūd

Lā Siyyama māhi 'lḥushūd; Saifu 'l'ilāh 'ibnu 'lwalīd

And the lions from the family and companions, became masters throuh him regardless of being white or black

Especially the one who wipes out great armys; the sword of god son of Alwalid

22 - Yā Tawāb Tub ʿAlayna

يَا تَوَّاب تُبْ عَلَيْنَا   ا وَارْحَمنَا وَانْظُرْ إلَينَا

Yā Tawāb tub ʿalayna   Wa 'rḥamnā wanẓur ilayna

O Forgiver, forgive us, And have mercy on us and look upon us 2x

(1) خُذْ يَمِينًا خُذْ يَمِينًا   عَنْ سَبِيلِ الظَّالِمِينَ

Khudh yamīnan khudh yamīnan ***ʿan sabīli 'ẓ-ẓālimīna***

Go right go right, Away from the path of oppressors

(2) واتّقِ اللّهَ تعالَى   عَنْ مَقَالِ المُلحِدِينَا

Wa 't-taqi 'l-lāha taʿālā ***ʿan maqāli 'l-mulḥidīnā***

And beware of Allāh, And leave the words of unbelievers

(3) الإلهُ الحَقُ رَبُّ العَرشِ   رَبُّ العَالَمِينَا

Al-Ilāhu 'l-Ḥaqqu Rabbu 'l-'Arshi ***Rabbu 'l-'ālamīnā***
Allāh the truth is the Lord of the Throne, The Lord of all worlds

(4) هُوَ رَبُّ الأوَّلِينَا   هُوَ رَبُّ الآخِرِينَا

Huwa Rabbu 'l-'awwalīna ***Huwa Rabbu 'l-'ākhirinā***
He is the Lord of the first ones, He is the Lord of the last ones

(5) هُوَ رَبِّي هُوَ حَسْبِي   هُوَ خَيرُ الرَّازِقِينَا

Huwa Rabbī huwa ḥasbīy ***Huwa khayru 'r-rāziqīnā***
He is my Lord he is my reliance, He is the best of grantors of sustenance

(6) هُوَ غَفَّارُ الخَطَايَا   هُوَ خَيْرُ الرَّاحِمِينَا

Huwa ghaffāru 'l-khaṭāyā ***Huwa khayru 'r-rāḥimīnā***
He is the forgiver of sins, He is the best of those who show mercy

(7) رَبي ادْخِلنَا جَمِيعًا   فِي العِبَادِ الصَّالِحِينَا

Rabbī adkhilnā jamī'an ***Fīl-'ibādi 'ṣ-ṣāliḥīnā***
My Lord let us enter the gardens, Amongst the righteous servants

(8) وَ ارْضَ عَنَّا وَ اعْفُ عَنَّا   وَ أجِرْنَا أَجْمَعِينَا

Wa 'arḍā 'annā wa'fū 'annā ***Wa ajirnā ajma'īnā***
And be pleased with us and forgive us, And safeguard all of us

(9) مِن عَذابٍ فِي جَحِيمٍ   أُرصِدَتْ لِلمُجْرِمِينَا

Min ʿadhābin fī jaḥīmin   Urṣidat li 'l-mujrimīnā
From a torment in the fire,   prepared for evildoers

(10) مِنْ عُصَاةٍ فَاسِقِينَا وَعُتَاةٍ كَافِرِينَا

Min ʿuṣātin fāsiqīna   Wa ʿutātin kāfirīnā
Of disobedient and corrupt ones,   And transgressing disbelievers

(11) رَبِّ أَدْخِلنَا جِنَانًا   أُزلِفَتْ لِلمُتَّقِينَا

Rabbī adkhilnā jinānan   Uzlifat li 'l-muttaqīnā
My Lord grant us to enter gardens,   Fashioned for the pious ones

(12) إِذْ يُنَادَونَ ادُخُلُوهَا   بِسَلَامٍ آمِنِينَا

Idh yunādūn 'dkhullūhā   Bi salāmin āminīnā
Where they will be told to enter, In peace and safety

(13) وَ صَلَاةُ اللهِ تَغشَى   أَحْمَدَ الهَادِي الأَمِينَا

Wa ṣalātulLāhi taghshā   Āḥmada 'l-hādi 'l-amīnā
And Allāh's blessings cover,   Ahmad the trustworthy guide

(14) وَ عَلَى آلِ وَ صَحبٍ   وَجَمِيعِ التَّابِعِينَا

Wa ʿalā ālin wa ṣaḥbi   Wa jamīʿi 't-tābiʿīnā
And his family and companions,   And all those who followed them

(15) مَا تَلَا تَالٍ قُرآنًا   جَاءَ بِالحَقِّ مُبِينَا

Mā talā tālin Qur'āna   Jā'a bi 'l-ḥaqqi mubīnā
Whenever a reciter recites Qur'an,   Which has brought the clear truth

اللهُمَّ صَلِّ وَسَلِّمْ وَبارِكْ عَلَيْهِ وَعلَىْ آلِه

Allāhuma ṣalli wa sallim wa bārik ʿalayhi wa ʿalā ālih

23 - Yā Rabbī Ṣalli ʿalā ʾn-Nabī Muḥammadin

يَا رَبِّ صَلِّ عَلَى النَّبِي مُحَمَّدٍ   خَيرِ الأَنَامِ وَ مَنْ بِهِ يُتَشفَّعُ

Yā Rabbī ṣalli ʿalā ʾn-Nabī Muḥammadin
Khayri ʾl-anāmi wa man bihi yutashaffaʿu 2x
My Lord send blessings upon the Prophet Muḥammad
The best of mankind whose intercessing means is sought

(1) يَا مَنْ يَرَىْ مَا فِي الضَّمِيرِ وَ يَسْمَعُ   أَنْتَ المُعَدُّ لِكُلِّ مَا يُتَوَقَّعُ

Yā man yarā mā fī ʾḍ-ḍamiri wa yasmaʿu
Anta ʾl-muʿaddu li-kulli mā yutawaqqaʿu
O you who sees and hears what's in the subconscious
You are our preparation for all things expected

(2) يَا مَنْ يُرَجَّى لِلشَدَائِدِ كُلِّهَا   يَا مَنْ إلَيْهِ المُشْتَكَىْ وَ المَفْزَعُ

Yā man yurajjā li-sh-shdāʾidi kulliha
Yā man ilayhi ʾl-mushtakā wa ʾl-mafzaʿu
O you who is sought after at times of all kinds of hardship
O you whom people confess their problems and you are a shelter for the fearful ones

(3) يَا مَنْ خَزَائِنُ مُلكِهِ فِيْ قَوْلِ كُن   أُمْنُنْ فَإنَّ الخَيرَ عِندَكَ أجْمَعُ

Yā man khazāʾinu mulkihi fī-qawli kun
Umnun fa-inna ʾl-khayra ʿindaka ajmaʿu
O you whose treasure chests are in his saying 'Be'
Grant us your favors because favors are contained in you

(4) مَا لِي سِوَى فَقْرِي إلَيكَ وَسيلَةٌ   فَبَالافتِقَارِ إليكَ فَقرِيَ أَدفَعُ

Mā lī siwā faqrī ilayka wasīlatun
Fabi ʾl-iftiqāri ilayka faqriya adfaʿu
My only means to you is my poverty
And through my poverty for you, I fend off poverty

(5) مَالِي سِوَى قَرْعِي لِبَابكَ حِيلَةٌ   فَلَئِـن رُدِدْتُ فَأيُّ بَابٍ أَقْرَعُ

Mā lī siwā qarʿī libābika ḥīlatun
Fa laʾin ruditdu fa ayyu bābin aqraʿu
I have nothing else except knocking at your door
If I am turned away, which door then can I knock on

(6) وَ مَنِ الَّذِي أَدْعُو وَ أَهْتِفُ بِاسْمِهِ   إِنْ كَانَ فَضْلُكَ عَنْ فَقِيرِكَ يُمْنَعُ

Wa mani 'l-ladhī adʿū wa ahtifu bismihi
In kāna faḍluk ʿan faqīrika yumnaʿu
And who else can I call upon and shout his name
If you kept your favors away from one who is poor for you

(7) حَاشَا لِجُودِكَ أَنْ تُقَنِّطَ عَاصِيًا   الْفَضْلُ أَجْزَلُ وَ الْمَوَاهِبُ أَوْسَعُ

Ḥashā li jūdika an ṭuqanniṭa ʿāṣiyan
Al-faḍlu ajzalu wa 'l-mawāhibu awsaʿu
As generous as you are, you would never hold back your bounty from a disobedient one
Your bounty is too abundant and your grants too vast for that

(8) ثُمَّ الصَّلاةُ عَلَى النَّبِي مُحَمَّدٍ   خَيرِ الأَنَامِ وَ مَنْ بِهِ يُتَشَفَّعُ

Thumm 'ṣ-ṣalatu ʿalā 'n-Nabī Muḥammadin
Khayri 'l-anāmi wa man bihi yutashaffaʿu
Then praise be upon the Prophet Muḥammad
The best of mankind and the means for intercession

اللهُمَّ صَلِّ وَسَلِّمْ وَبَارِكْ عَلَيْهِ وَعَلَىٰ آلِه

Allāhuma ṣalli wa sallim wa bārik ʿalayhi wa ʿalā ālih

24 - An-Nabī Ṣallū ʿAlayh

النَّبِيّ صلُّوا عَلَيْه – صلُّوا عَلَيْه
An-nabī ṣallū ʿalayh, ṣallu ʿalayh
صَلَوَاتُ اللهِ عَلَيه– صلَّى اللهُ عَلَيه
Ṣalawātullāhi ʿalayh, ṣall-Allāhu ʿalayh
وَيَنَالُ البَرَكَاتْ – البَرَكَاتْ
Wa yanālu ʾl-barakāt, al-barakāt
كُلُّ مَنْ صَلَّى عَلَيْه– صلَّى اللهُ عَليه

(1) مَرْحَبًا يَا نُورَ عَينِي مَرحَبًا

Marḥaban yā nūra ʿaynī, marḥaba
Welcome! O light of my eye, welcome!

(2) مَرْحَبًا يَا مَرْحَبًا أَلْفَي مَرحَبًا

Marḥaban yā marḥaban alfay marḥaba
Welcome! O welcome! A thousand welcomes!

(3) مَرْحَبًا جَدَّ الحُسَيْنِ مَرحَبًا

Marḥaban jadda ʾl-Ḥusayni marḥaba
Welcome! O grandfather of al-Ḥusayn, welcome!

(4) مَرْحَبًا يَا مَرْحَبًا أَلْفَي مَرحَبًا

Marḥaban Yā marḥaban alfay marḥaba
Welcome! O welcome! A thousand welcomes!

(5) النَّبِيّ صلُّوا عَلَيْه – صلُّوا عَلَيْه

An-nabī ṣallū ʿalayh, ṣallū ʿalayh
Send praise upon the Prophet, send praise!

(6) صَلَوَاتُ اللهِ عَلَيه – صلَّى اللهُ عَلَيه

ṢalawātulLāhi ʿalayh, ṣall-Allāhu ʿalayh
Allāh's blessings upon him, upon him

(7) وَيَنَالُ البَرَكَاتْ — البَرَكَاتْ

Wa yanālu 'l-barakāt, al-barakāt
He will receive blessings, blessings

(8) كُلُّ مَنْ صَلَّى عَلَيْه — صَلَّى اللهُ عَلَيه

Kullu man ṣallā 'alayh, ṣall-Allāhu 'alayh
Whoever asks blessing on him, Allāh will send blessings too

(9) النَّبِيّ يَا مَنْ حَضَرْ — يَا مَنْ حَضَرْ

An-nabī yā man ḥaḍar, yā man ḥaḍar
The Prophet, O attendees, O attendees

(10) النَّبِيّ خَيْرُ البَشَرْ — خَيْرُ البَشَرْ

An-nabī khayru 'l-bashar, khayru 'l-bashar
The Prophet is the best of humans, best of humans

(11) مَنْ دَنَا لَهُ القَمَرْ — لَهُ القَمَرْ

Man danā lahu 'l-qamar, lahu 'l-qamar
He's the one for whom the moon came down, moon came down

(12) وَالغَزَالْ سَلَّمْ عَلِيهْ — صَلَّى اللهُ عَلَيه

Wa 'l-ghazāl sallam 'alayh, ṣall-Allāhu 'alayh
And the gazelle greeted him, Allāh sent blessings upon him

(13) النَّبِيّ ذَاكَ الْعَرُوسْ — ذَاكَ الْعَرُوسْ

An-nabī dhāka 'l-'arūs, dhāka 'l-'arūs
The Prophet is the bridegroom, the bridegroom

(14) ذِكْرُهُ يُحْيِي النُّفُوسْ — يُحْيِي النُّفُوسْ

Dhikruhu yuḥyī 'n-nufūs, yuḥyī 'n-nufūs
Mentioning him gives life to the soul, life to the soul

(15) النَّصَارَىْ وَالمَجُوسْ — قُلْ وَالمَجُوسْ

An-naṣāra wa 'l-majūs, qul wa 'l-majūs
The Christians and the Zoroastrians, the Zoroastrians

(16) أَسْلَمُوا عَلَى يَدَيْهْ — صَلَّى اللهُ عَلَيه

Aslamū 'alā yadayh, Ṣall-Allāhu 'alayh
accepted Islam because of him, Allāh sent blessings upon him

(17) النَّبيّ ذَاكَ المَلِيحْ – ذَاكَ المَلِيحْ

An-nabī dhāka 'l-malīḥ, dhāka 'l-malīḥ
The Prophet who is very fine, very fine

(18) قَوْلُهُ قَوْلٌ فَصِيحْ – قَوْلٌ فَصِيحْ

Qawluhu qawlun faṣīḥ, qawlun faṣīḥ
His words are very articulate, very articulate

(19) وَالقُرآن شَيئٌ صَحِيحْ – شَيئٌ صَحِيحْ

Wa 'l-Qur'ān shay'un ṣaḥīḥ, shay'un ṣaḥīh
And the Qur'an is a true book, a true book

(20) الذِّيْ أُنزِلْ عَلَيهْ – صلَّى اللهُ عَلَيه

Al-ladhī unzil 'alayh, ṣall-Allāhu 'alayh
it was revealed to him, Allāh sent blessings upon him

(21) النَّبيّ يَا حَاضِرين – يَا حَاضِرين

An-nabī yā ḥāḍirīn. Yā ḥāḍirīn
The Prophet, O attendees, O attendees!

(22) إعْلَمُوا عِلْمَ اليَقِين – عِلْمَ اليَقِين

I'lamū 'ilma 'l-yaqīn, 'ilma 'l-yaqīn
Know with certainty, with certainty

(23) أَنَّ رَبَّ العَالَمِين – العَالَمِين

Anna rabba 'l-'ālamīn, al-'ālamīn
That the Lord of all the worlds, all the worlds

(24) أَفرَضَ الصَّلاةَ عَلَيهْ – صلَّى اللهُ عَلَيه

Afraḍa 'ṣ-ṣalāt 'alayh, ṣall-Allāh 'alayh
Made praising him an obligation, O Allāh send blessings upon him

(25) النَّبيّ الْمُجْتَبَىْ – الْمُجْتَبَىْ

An-nabiyyu 'l-mujtabā, al-mujtabā
The Prophet who was collected, who was collected

(26) الذِّيْ نَزَلْ قُبَا – نَزَلْ قُبَا

Alladhī nazal qubā, nazal qubā
Who stayed at Qubā, stayed at Qubā

(27) اَظْهَرَ الدِّينَ وْنَبَا – قل وْنَبَا

Aẓhar 'd-dīna wa nabā, qul wa nabā
He spread the religion and gave the news, the news

(28) كُلُّكُمْ صَلُّوْا عَلِيه – صَلَّى اللهُ عَلَيه

Kullukum ṣallū 'alayh, ṣall-Allāhu 'alayh
All of you praise him, Allāh sent blessings upon him

(29) النَّبِيّ المُصْطَفَى – المُصْطَفَى

An-nabīyyu 'l-Muṣṭafā, al-Muṣṭafā
The prophet who is the chosen one, the chosen one

(30) ابنُ زَمْزَمْ وَالصَّفَا – زَمْزَمْ وَالصَّفَا

Ibnu zamzam wa 'ṣ-ṣafā, zamzam wa 'ṣ-ṣafā
The son of Zamzam and Ṣafā, Zamzam and Ṣafā

(31) مَنْ تَعَالَى شَرَفًا – قلْ شَرَفًا

Man ta'ālā sharafā, qul sharafā
Whose honor is exalted, his honor

(32) كُلُّكُمْ صَلُّوا عَلَيهْ – صَلَّى اللهُ عَلَيه

Kullukum ṣallū 'alayh, ṣall-Allāhu 'alayh
All of you praise him, O Allāh send blessings upon him

(33) وَامْتَدِحْ زَوجَ البَتُوْل – زَوجَ البَتُوْل

Wamtadiḥ zawja 'l-batūl, zawja 'l-batūl
and praise the husband of al-Batūl (Fatima), the husband of al-Batūl

(34) إبْنُ عَمٍ لِلْرَسُوْل – قُلْ لِلْرَسُوْل

Ibnu 'ammin li 'r-rasūl, qul li 'r-rasūl
The cousin of the Messenger, the Messenger

(35) مَنْ أَحْبَبْهُمْ فِيْ قَبُولْ – قُلْ فِيْ قَبُولْ

Man aḥbabhum fī qabūl, qul fī qabūl
Whoever loves them will be accepted, accepted

(36) وَالإِلَهْ يَرْضَى عَلَيهْ – صَلَّى اللهُ عَلَيه

Wa 'l-ilāh yarḍā 'alayh, ṣall-Allāhu 'alayh
And Allāh will be pleased with him, Allāh sent blessings upon him

(37) الْحَسَنْ ثُمَّ الْحُسَينْ – ثُمَّ الْحُسَينْ

Al-Ḥasan thumma 'l-Ḥusayn, thumma 'l-Ḥusayn
Ḥasan and then Ḥusayn, and then Ḥusayn

(38) لِلْنَّبِّي قُرَّةُ عَينْ – قُرَّةُ عَينْ

Li 'n-nabī qurratu 'ayn , qurratu 'ayn
Are the coolness of the Prophet's eyes, coolness

(39) نُورُهُمْ كَالْكَوكَبَينْ — كَالْكَوكَبَينْ

Nūruhum ka 'l-kawkabayn, ka 'l-kawkabayn
Their lights like two planets, shining, like two planets

(40) جَدُّهُم صَلُّوا عَلَيهْ – صَلَّى اللّهُ عَلَيه

Jadduhum ṣallū 'alayh, ṣall-Allāhu 'alayh
Send praising upon their grandfather, Allāh sent blessings upon him

(41) أَبُو بَكْرٍ وَعُمَرْ — قُلْ وَعُمَرْ

Abū Bakrin wa 'Umar, qul wa 'Umar
Abū Bakr and 'Umar, and 'Umar

(42) نُورُهُم يَعلُوا القَمَرْ – يَعلُوا القَمَرْ

Nūruhum ya'lū 'l-qamar, ya'lū 'l-qamar
Their light overcomes the light of the moon

(43) مَنْ أَبْغَضهُم فِيْ سَقَر — قُلْ فِيْ سَقَر

Man abghaḍahum fī saqar, qul fī saqar
Whoever hates them may end in hell, in hell

(44) والإِلَه يَسخَطْ عَليه – يَسخَطْ عَليه

Wa 'l-ilāh yaskhaṭ 'alayh, yaskhaṭ 'alayh
And God will be angry with him, angry with him

(45) وَتَرَضُّوا عَن ذِي النُّورَين – عَن ذِي النُّورَين

Wa taraḍḍū 'an dhi'n-nūrayn, 'an dhi'n-nūrayn
May Allāh be pleased with the Possessor of the two lights, two lights

(46) مَنْ تَزَوَّجْ قَمَريْن — قُلْ قَمَريْن

Man tazawwaj qamarayn, qul qamarayn
Who had married two moons (the daughters of the Prophet), two moons

(47) مَن تَرَضَّى فِي خَيرَين – قُلْ فِي خَيرَين

Man taraḍḍā fī khayrayn, qul fī khayrayn
Whoever asks Allāh to be pleased with him receive two goodnesses

(48) وَالمَولَى يَرضَى عَليهْ – يَرضَى عَليهْ

Wa 'l-Mawlā yarḍā ʿalayh, yarḍā ʿalayh
And the Lord will be pleased with him

(49) النَّبيّ صلُّوا عَلَيْه – صلُّوا عَلَيْه

An-nabī ṣallū ʿalayh, ṣallu ʿalayh
Send praise upon the Prophet, send praise

(50) صَلَوَاتُ اللهِ عَلَيه – صلَّى اللهُ عَلَيه

ṢalawātulLāhi ʿalayh, ṣall-Allāhu ʿalayh
Allāh's blessings upon the Prophet, Allāh blessings on him

(51) وَيَنَالُ البَرَكَاتْ – البَرَكَاتْ

Wa yanālu 'l-barakāt, al-barakāt
He will receive blessings, blessings

(52) كُلُّ مَنْ صَلَّى عَلَيْه – صلَّى اللهُ عَلَيه

Kullu man ṣalla ʿalayh, ṣall-Allāhu ʿalayh
Whoever asks blessing on him, Allāh will bless too

اللهُمَّ صَلِّ وَسَلِّمْ وَبَارِكْ عَلَيْهِ وَعَلَىْ آلِه

Allāhuma ṣallī wa sallim wa bārik ʿalayhi wa ʿalā ʿālih

25 - Yā Badra Timma

اللهُمَّ صَلِّ وَسَلِّمْ وَبَارِكْ عَلَيْهِ وَعلَىْ آلِه

Allāhuma ṣallī wa sallim wa bārik ʿalayhi wa ʿalā ʿālih

(1) يا بَدرُ تَمَّ فَحازَ كُلَّ كَمالِ   ماذَا يُعَبِّرُ عَنْ عُلاكَ مَقَالِيْ

Yā badru tamma faḥāza kulla kamāli
mādhā yuʿabbiru ʿan ʿulāka maqālī
O full moon that has achieved all perfection,
How can my words describe your high status?

(2) أَنْتَ الَّذِيْ أَشرَقْتَ فِيْ أُفُقِ الْعُلاَ   فَمَحَوْتَ بِالأَنْوَارِ كُلَّ ضَلاَلِ

Anta ʾlladhī ashraqta fi ufuqi ʾl-ʿulā
Fa-maḥawta bi ʾl-anwāri kulla ḍalāli
You are the one that rose above the high horizon,
With your light, you erased all falsehood,

(3) وَبِكَ اسْتَنَارَ الكَوْنُ يا عَلَمَ الْهُدَىْ   بِالنُّورِ وَالإِنْعَامِ وَالإِفْضَالِ

Wa bika ʾstanāra ʾl-kawnu yā ʿalama ʾl-hudā
bi ʾn-nūri wa ʾl-inʿāmi wa ʾl-ifḍāli
O Banner of Guidance, because of you the universe
is lit up with lights, gifts and favors,

(4) صَلَّىْ عَلَيْكَ اللهُ رَبِّيْ دَائِمًا   أَبَداً مَعَ الإِبْكَارِ وَالآصَالِ

Ṣallā ʿalayka Allāhu Rabbī dāʾiman
abadan maʿa ʾl-ibkāri wa ʾl-ʾĀṣāl
Our Lord, Allāh, bestowed blessings upon you
Eternally in the early morning and evening.

(5) وَعَلَىْ جَمِيعِ الآلِ وَالأَصحَابِ مَنْ   قَدْ خَصَّهُمْ رَبُّ العُلاَ بِكَمَالِ

Wa ʿalā jamīʿi ʾl-ʾāli wa ʾl-aṣḥābi min
qad khaṣṣahum rabbu ʾl-ʿulā bi-kamāli
And upon all your family and companions,
the Lord the Most High, specialized them with perfection.

26 - Yā Imāma 'r-Rusli

يَا إِمَامَ الرُّسْلِ يَا سَنَدِي أَنتَ بَابُ اللهِ مُعْتَمَدِي

فَبِدُنيَايَ وَآخِرَتِي يَا رَسُولَ اللهِ خُذْ بِيَدِي

Yā imāma 'r-rusli yā sanadī anta bābu 'l-lāhi mu'tamadī
Fa bi-dunyāya wa 'ākhiratī yā rasulalLāhi khudh bi-yadī

Oh Leader of the messengers, O my support, you are Allah's door, on whom I relie
In my life and in my hereafter, O Messenger of Allah! Hold my hand.

(1) قَسَمًا بِالنَّجْمِ حِينَ هَوَى مَا المُعَافَى وَالسَّقِيمُ سَوَى

(2) فَاخْلَعِ الكَونَينِ عَنكَ سِوَى حُبِّ مَولَى العُربِ وَالعَجَمِ

Qasaman bi 'n-najmi ḥīna hawā mā 'l-mu'āfa wa 's-saqīmu sawā
fakhla'i 'l-kawnayni 'anka siwa ḥubbi mawla 'l-'urbi wa 'l-'ajami

By the star in descent, I swear, the healthy and the sick are not equal,
So doff both worlds from you except the love of the master of the Arabs and non Arabs

(3) سَيِّدُ السَادَاتِ مِن مُضَرِ غَوثُ اَهلِ البَدوِ وَالحَضَرِ

(4) صَاحِبُ الآيَاتِ وَالسُّوَرِ مَنْبَعُ الْأَحْكَامِ وَالحِكَمِ

Sayyidu 's-sādāti min muḍari ghawthu ahli 'l-badwi wa 'l-ḥaḍari
ṣāḥibu 'l-'āyāti wa 's-suwari manba'u 'l-aḥkāmi wa 'l-ḥikami

Master of masters from Muḍari, Succor of Bedouins and urbane folk
Owner of the verses and chapters, springbed of laws and wisdom

(5) قَمَرٌ طَابَتْ سَرِيرَتُه وَسَجَايَاهُ وَسِيرَتُهُ

(6) صَفْوَةُ الْبَارِي وَخِيرَتُهُ عِدلُ أهلِ الحِلِّ وَالحَرَمِ

qamarun ṭābat sarīratuhu wa sajāyāhu wa sīratuhu
ṣafwatu 'l-bārī wa khīratuhu 'idlu ahli 'l-ḥilli wa 'l-ḥarami

A moon possessing good essence, good nature and good name
Purest elect of the Creator and His ultimate choice, best of both upright and wrongdoing folk

(7) مَا رَأَتْ عَينٌ وَلَيسَ تَرَى   مِثلَ طَهَ فِي الوَرَى بَشَرَ

(8) خَيرُ مَنْ مَسَّ الثَرَى أثَرَ   طَاهِرُ الأَخلاقِ وَالشِّيَمِ

mā ra'at 'aynun wa laysa tarā ***mithla ṭāhā fi 'l-warā bashara***

khayru man massa 'th-tharā 'athara ***ṭāhiru 'l-akhlāqi wa 'sh-shīyyami***

No eye has seen nor will eye ever see, the like of Ṭāhā among humanity

With the best life story of those resting below, purer of conduct and quality no like is found.

اللهُمَّ صَلِّ وَسَلِّمْ وَبَارِكْ عَلَيْهِ وَعلَىْ آلِه

Allāhuma ṣalli wa sallim wa bārik 'alayhi wa 'alā ālih

27 - Aṣ-Ṣalātu 'l-Badrīyyah

صَلاةُ اللهِ سَلامُ اللهِ   عَلَى طَهَ رَسُولِ اللهِ
صَلاةُ اللهِ سَلامُ اللهِ   عَلَى يَس حَبِيبِ اللهِ

Ṣalātullāh salāmullāh   ***ʿalā Ṭāhā rasūlillāh***
Ṣalātullāh salāmullāh   ***ʿalā yāsīn ḥabībillāh***
Allah's praise, Allah's blessing   upon Tāhā, Prophet of Allah
Allah's praise, Allah's blessing,   upon the YāSīn, Beloved of Allah

(1) تَوَسَّلنَا بِبِسمِ اللهِ   وَبِالهَادِي رَسُولِ اللهِ
(2) وَكُلِّ مُجَاهِدٍ لِلّهِ   بِأَهْلِ البَدرِ يَا اَللهِ

Tawassalnā bi-bismillāh   ***wa bi 'l-hādī rasūlillāh***
Wa kulli mujāhidin lillāh   ***bi ahli 'l-badri yā Allāh***
We sought by means of *bismillāh*   and by the Guide, God's Messenger
And everyone striving in God's Way,   by means of the full moon's family (Prophet Muhammad ﷺ) O Allāh!

(3) اِلَهِي سَلِّمِ الأُمَّةَ   مِنَ الآفَاتِ وَالنِّقمَةَ
(4) وَمِن هَمٍّ وَمِن غُمَّةْ   بِأَهْلِ البَدرِ يَا اَللهِ

Ilāhi sallimi 'l-umma   ***mina 'l-'āfāti wa 'n-niqmah***
Wa min hammin wa min ghummah   ***bi ahli 'l-badri yā Allāh***
My God grant safety to the nation   from diseases and retribution
And from worries and from sadness   by means of the full moon's family, O Allāh!

(5) اِلَهِي نَجِّنَا وَاكشِفْ   جَمِيعَ أَذِيَّةٍ وَاصرِفْ
(6) مَكَائِدَ العِدَا وَالطُف   بِأَهْلِ البَدرِ يَا اَللهِ

Ilāhi najjinā w 'akshif   ***jamīʿa 'adhiyyatin wa aṣrif***
makāʿidal ʿidā wa 'lṭuf   ***bi āhli 'l-badri yā Allāh***
My God save us and lift   all harm from us, and ward off
our enemies' schemes from us,   by means of the full moon's family O Allāh!

(7) اِلَهي نَفِّسِ الكُرَبَا   مِنَ العَاصِينَ وَالعَطبَا

(8) وَكُلِّ بَلِيَّةٍ وَوَبَاءْ   بأهْلِ البَدرِ يا اَللّه

ilāhi naffisi 'l-kurabā	***mina 'l-'āsīna wa 'l-'aṭbā***
wa kulli balīyyatin wa wabā'	***bi ahli 'l-badri yā Allāh***
My God relieve the distress	from the disobedient and corrupt,
from every trial and epidemic,	by means of the full moon's family, O Allāh!

(9) فَكَمْ مِن رَحمَةٍ حَصَلَت   وَكَمْ مِنْ ذِلَّةٍ فَصَلَتْ

(10) وَكَمْ مِنْ نِعمَةٍ وَصَلَت   بأهْلِ البَدرِ يَا اَللّه

fakam min raḥmatin ḥaṣalat	***wa kam min dhillatin faṣalat***
wa kam min ni'matin waṣalat	***bi ahli 'l-badri yā Allāh***
How many mercies have occurred!	And how many humiliations were lifted!
And how many favors have been granted!	by means of the full moon's family, O Allāh!

(11) وَكَم أوْلَيتَ ذَا العُمرِ   وَكَمْ أغنَيتَ ذَا الفَقرِ

(12) وَكَمْ عَافَيتَ ذَا الوِزرِ   بأهْلِ البَدرِ يَا اَللّه

Wa kam 'aghnayta dha 'l-faqri	***wa kam awlayta dha 'l-'umri***
Wa kam 'āfayta dha 'l-wizri	***bi ahli 'l-badri yā Allāh***
How many a poor one have You sustained?	How many old ones have You cared for?
How many burdened ones have you healed!	by means of the full moon's Family, O Allāh!

(13) لَقَد ضَاقَت عَلى القَلبِ   جَميعَ الأَرضِ والرَحبِ

(14) فَانْجُ مِنَ البَلا الصَعبِ   بأهْلِ البَدرِ يَا اَللّه

laqad ḍāqat 'ala 'l-qalbi	***jamī'u 'l-arḍi ma' raḥbi***
f'anji mina 'l-balā 'ṣ-ṣa'bi	***bi ahli 'l-badri yā Allāh***
The earth with all its vastness	has constricted the heart,
so save yourself from the difficult ordeal,	by means of the full moon's family O Allāh!

(15) أتينا طَالِبي الرِّفقِ وَجُلّ الخَيرِ وَالسَّعدِ

(16) فَوَسِّع مِنحَةَ الأيْدي بِأهْلِ البَدرِ يَا اَللّه

ataynā ṭālibī 'r-rafqi *wa julli 'l-khayri wa 's-saʿdi*
fawassaʿ minḥata 'l-aydī *bi ahli 'l-badri yā Allāh*
We came here asking mercy and abundance of goodness and joy,
so expand your grants, by means of the full moon's family,
O Allāh!

(17) فَلا تَردُدْ مَع الخَيبَة بَلِ اجعَلنَا عَلَى الطَّيبَة

(18) أيَا ذَا العِزِّ وَالهَيبَة بِأهْلِ البَدرِ يَا اَللّه

falā tardud maʿ al-khayba *bali 'jʿalnā ʿalā aṭ-ṭayba*
ayā dha 'l-ʿizzi wa 'l-hayba *bi ahli 'l-badri yā Allāh*
So turn us not back disheartened, rather let us achieve goodness
O Honored One full of Majesty, by means of the full moon's family,
O Allāh!

(19) وَإنْ تَردُدْ فَمَنْ نَأتِي بِنَيلِ جَمِيعِ حَاجَاتِي

(20) أيَا جَالِي المُلِمَّاتِ بِأهْلِ البَدرِ يَا اَللّه

wa in tardud faman na'tī *binayli jamīʿi ḥājātī*
ayā jālī 'l-mulimmāti *bi ahli 'l-badri yā Allāh*
If You rebuff us to whom shall we go for all our needs?
O one who washes away hardship, by means of the full moon's family,
O Allāh!

(21) إلَهِي اغفِر وَاكرِمنَا بِنَيلِ مَطالِبٍ مِنَّا

(22) وَدَفعِ مَسَاءَةٍ عَنَّا بِأهْلِ البَدرِ يَا اَللّه

Ilāhī 'ghfir wa 'akrimnā *binayli maṭālibin minnā*
wa dafʿī masā'atin ʿanna *bi ahli 'l-badri yā Allāh*
My God forgive and honor us, by granting us our requests,
and fending harm from us, by means of the full moon's family,
O Allāh!

(23) اِلَهِي أنتَ ذُو لُطفٍ وَذُو فَضلٍ وَذُو عَطفٍ

(24) وَكَمْ مِنْ كُرُبَةٍ تَنفِي بِأهْلِ البَدرِ يَا اَللهْ

Ilāhī anta dhu luṭfin ***wa dhu faḍlin wa dhu ʿaṭfin***
Wa kam min kurbatin tanfī ***bi ahli ʾl-badri yā Allāh***

My God you are Tender, Dispenser of favors, and compassionate.
How many hardships have You lifted, by means of the full moon's family, O Allāh!

(25) وَصَلِّ عَلَى النَّبِي البَرِّ بِلا عَدٍ وَلا حَصرِ

(26) وَآلِ سَادَةٍ غُرِّ بِأهْلِ البَدرِ يَا اَللهْ

Wa ṣallī ʿalā ʾn-nabī ʾl-barri ***bilā ʿaddin wa lā ḥaṣri***
wa ālin sādatin ghurri ***bi ahli ʾl-badri yā Allāh***

And send Your blessings upon the righteous prophet, without count and with no limit,
and on the distinguished masters of his family, by means of the full moon's family, O Allāh!

اللهُمَّ صَلِّ وَسَلِّمْ وَبَارِكْ عَلَيْهِ وَعَلَىْ آلِه

Allāhuma ṣalli wa sallim wa bārik ʿalayhi wa ʿalā ālih

28 - Alfu Salām

صَلاةٌ مِنَ اللهِ وَألفُ سَلامْ عَلَى المُصطَفَى احمَدْ شَرِيفِ المَقَامْ
صَلاةٌ مِنَ اللهِ وَألفُ سَلامْ عَلَى المُصطَفَى احمَدْ شَرِيفِ المَقَامْ

Ṣalātun min-Allāh wa alfu salām ʿala ʾl-Muṣṭafa ʾAḥmad sharīfi ʾl-maqām
Ṣalātun min-Allāh wa alfu salām ʿala ʾl-Muṣṭafa ʾAḥmad sharīfi ʾl-maqām
God's Peace and blesssings and thousands of praise, upon Āḥmad the Chosen whose station's on high

(1) سَلامٌ سَلامٌ كَمِسكِ الخِتَامِ عَلَيكُم أُحَيبَابَنَا يَا كِرَامْ
(2) وَمَنْ ذِكرُهُمْ اُنسُنَا فِي الظَّلامِ وَنُورٌ لَنَا بَينَ هَذَا الأَنَامْ

Salāmun salāmun ka-miski ʾl-khitām ʿalaykum uḥaybā-banā yā kirām
Wa man dhikruhum unsunā fi ʾẓ-ẓalām wa nūrun lanā bayn hādhā ʾl-anām
Greetings of peace scented with musk, upon you most be-loved and honored of folk
Your mention is solace for us in dark times, and a light shining forth in creation for us

(3) سَكَنتُمْ فُؤادِي وَربِّ العِبَادْ وَأنتُم مُنَائِي وَاقصَى المُرَاد
(4) فَهَل تُسعِدُونِي بِصَفوِ الوِدَادِ وَهَلْ تَمنَحُونِي شَرِيْفَ المَقَامْ

Sakantum fuʾādi wa rabbi ʾl-ʿibād wa antum munāʾī wa aqṣā ʾl-murād
Fa-hal tusʿidūnī bi-ṣafwi ʾl-widād wa hal tamnaḥūnī sharīfa ʾl-maqām
By the Lord of all servants, you dwell in my heart, you are whom I seek and the highest of aims.
So will you by pure love, give me great joy, and grant me to see the one who Has a high station?

(5) أنَا عَبدُكُم يَا أُهَيلَ الْوَفَا وَفِي قُربِكُم مَرهَمِي وَالشِّفَا
(6) فَلا تُسقِمُونِي بِطُولِ الجَفَا وَمُنُّوا بِوَصْلٍ وَلَو فِي المَنَامْ

Anā ʿabdukum yā uhayla ʾl-wafā wa fī qurbikum marhamī wa ʾsh-shifā
Falā tusqimūnī biṭūli ʾl-jafā wa munnū bi-waṣlin wa law fi ʾl-manām
I am your servant, O folk of loyalty, and closeness to you is my tonic and cure
So let me not whither by long shunning me, and grant that I see you, if only in dreams.

(7) اَمُوتُ وَأحيَا عَلى حُبِّكُم   وَذُلِّي لَديكم وَعِزِّي بِكم

(8) ورَاحَاتُ رُوحِي رَجَا قُربكُم   وَعَزمِي وَقَصدِي اِليكُم دَوَامْ

Amūtu wa aḥyā ʿalā ḥubbikum ***wa dhullī ladaykum wa ʿizzībikum***
Wa rāḥātu rūḥī rajā qurbikum ***wa ʿazmī wa qaṣdī ilaykum dawām***

I die and I live by my love of you, my humility is in your hands and so is my honor,
my soul's peace depends on closeness to you, my effort and aim is nearness to you.

(9) فَلا عِشتُ اِنْ كَانَ قَلبِي سَكَنْ   اِلَى الْبُعدِ عَنْ أهْلِهِ وَالوَطَنْ

(10) وَمَنْ حُبُّهُمْ فِي الحَشَا قَدْ قَطَنْ   وَخَامَرَ مِنِّي جَمِيعَ العِظَامْ

Fa lā ʿishtu in kāna qalbī sakan ***ilā 'l-buʿdi ʿan ahlihi wa 'l-waṭan***
Wa man ḥubbuhum fi 'l-ḥashā qad qaṭan ***wa khāmara minnī jamīʿa 'l-ʿiẓām***

I wish not to live with a heart is at ease, with being far from family and home
And those whose love has resided in my core, and penetrated all my bones

(11) إذَا مَرَّ بِالقَلبِ ذِكْرُ الحَبِيبِ   وَوَادِي العَقِيقِ وَذَاكَ الكَثِيبْ

(12) يَمِيلُ كَمَيلِ القَضِيبِ الْرَطِيبْ   وَيَهتَزُّ مِنْ شَوقِهِ وَالغَرَامْ

Idhā marra bi 'l-qalbi dhikru 'l-ḥabīb ***wa wādī 'l-ʿaqīqi wa dhāka 'l-kathīb***
Yamīlu kamayli 'l-qaḍībi 'l-raṭīb ***wa yahtazu min shawqihi wa 'l-gharām***

If the beloved's remembrance strolled through the heart, and the Valley of Turquoise and that glorious dune
It would lean like a green branch (awave in the wind), and shake from its yearning and from its great love.

(13) اَمُوتُ وَمَا زُرتُ ذَاكَ الغِنَا   وَتِلكَ الخِيامَ وَفِيهَا المُنَى

(14) وَلَمْ ادنُ يَومًا مَع مَنْ دَنَا   لِلَثْمِ المُحَيَّا وَشُربِ المُدَامْ

Amūtu wa mā zurtu dhāka 'l-ghinā ***wa tilka 'l-khiyāma wa fīhā 'l-munā***
Wa lam adnu yawman maʿa man danā ***li lathmi 'l-muḥaya wa shurbi 'l-mudām***

I die without visiting that treasure-house, and that tent in which lies my hope
And I did not draw near with those who approached, In order to cover my shame and drink the nectar of love.

(15) لَئِنْ كَانَ هَذَا فَيَا غُربَتِي   وَيَا طُولَ حُزنِي وَيَا كُربَتِي

(16) وَلِي حُسنُ ظَنٍّ بِهِ قُرْبَتِي   بِرَبِّي وَحَسبِي بِهِ يَا غُلامْ

la'in kāna hādhā fa yā ghurbatī ***wa yā ṭūla ḥuznī wa yā kurbatī***
wa lī ḥusnu ẓannin bihi qurbatī ***bi-rabbī wa ḥasbī bihi ya ghulām***

If this is my lot, o what a stranger I am, then what endless sadness and pain that would be,
But my kinship to him my hope keeps alive, and trust in my Lord and in him, O my child.

(17) عَسَى اللهُ يَشفِي غَلِيلَ الصُّدُودِ   بِوَصلِ الحَبَائِبْ وَفَكِّ القُيُودْ

(18) فَرَبِّي رَحِيمٌ كَرِيمٌ وَدُودٌ   يَجُودُ عَلَى مَنْ يَشَا بِالمَرَامْ

ʿasā 'lLāhu yashfī ghalīla 'ṣ-ṣudūd ***bi-waṣli 'l-ḥabā'ib wa fakki 'l-quyūd***
Fa rabbī raḥīmun karīmun wadūd ***yajūdu ʿalā man yashā' bi 'l-marām***

May God heal the burning of being denied nearness , by connecting us with loved ones and freeing the chains
My merciful, generous and all-loving Lord, grants whom He wishes whatever they want.

اللهُمَّ صَلِّ وَسَلِّمْ وَبَارِكْ عَلَيْهِ وَعلَىْ آلِه

Allāhuma ṣalli wa sallim wa bārik ʿalayhi wa ʿalā ʿālih

29 - Ḥusni 'l-Khātimah

يَا اللّٰه بِهَا يَاللّٰه بِهَا   يَاللّٰه بِحُسنِ الخَاتِمَة

Yā Allāh biha, Yā Allāh biha, Yā Allāh bi-ḥusni 'l-khātimah

Oh Allāh grant us, oh Allāh grant us, grant us a good ending

(1) لِي عَشرَةٌ أُطْفِي بِهِمْ   نَارَ الجَحِيمِ الحَاطِمَةْ

Lī ʿashratun uṭfī bihim ***nāra 'l-jaḥīmi 'l-ḥāṭimah***

I have ten means by which I to extinguish the fire which destroys (hell):

(2) المُصطَفَى وَالمُرتَضَى   وَابنَاهُمَا وَفَاطِمَةْ

Al-Muṣṭafā wal-Murtaḍā ***wa 'abnāhumā wa Fāṭimah***

The Chosen One (Muḥammad ﷺ), the satisfied one (ʿAlī ؓ), their two children (Ḥasan and Ḥusayn)and Fāṭimah ؓ;

(3) وَخَدِيجَةَ الكُبرَى الَّتِي   هِي لِلمَعَالِي خَاتِمَةْ

Wa Khadījata 'l-kubrā allatī ***hiya li 'l-maʿālī khātimah***

And the great Khadijah ؓ who reached the highest honors;

(4) وَبِعَائِشَةَ ذَاتِ الجَمَال   أُمِّ الكَمَال العَالِمَةْ

Wa biʿāʾishah dhāti 'l-jamāl ***ummi 'l-kamāli 'l-ʿālimah***

And through ʿĀʾisha the beautiful one, the mother of perfection and the scholar.

(5) وَبِبِنتِ عُمرَانَ أُمِّ عِيسَى   لَم تَزَل لِي رَاحِمَةْ

Wa bi-binti ʿumrāna ummi ʿĪsā ***lam tazal lī rāḥimah***

and through the daughter of Imran the mother of Jesus who is still merciful to me.

(6) وَبِآسِيَة مَنْ اَصبَحَتْ   مِنْ كُلِّ هَول سَالِمَة

Wa bi 'Āsiyata man aṣbaḥat ***min kulli hawlin sālimah***

And through Āsīyah who reached safety from all affliction;

(7) وَبِحَقِّ جِبرِيلَ الأَمِينَ   عَلى الصَحَائِفِ تَآمَة

Wa bi-ḥaqqi Jibrīl al-amīn ***ʿalā 'ṣ-ṣaḥāʾifi tāmah***

And through Jibrīl who is entrusted over all the books.

(8) هُمْ خِيرَتِي وَذَخِيرَتِي   فِي الحَشْرِ يَومَ الطَّامَّةْ

Hum khīratī wa dhakhīratī ***fī 'l-ḥashri yawma 'ṭ-ṭāmmah***
They are my goodness and my supplies, on the Day of the overwhelming Gathering

(9). وَكَذَاكَ فِي الدُّنيَا إِذَا   جَاءَتِ الخُطُوبِ القَاسِمَة

Wa kadhāka fi 'd-dunyā idhā ***jā'ati 'l-khuṭūbi 'l-qāsimah***
Also in this life when the back-breaking difficulty arrives

(10) وَبِحَقِّهِم يَا ذَا الجَلَال   وَبِالصَّلَاةِ القَائِمَةْ

Wa bi-ḥaqqihim yā dha 'l-jalāl ***wa bi 'ṣ-ṣalāti 'l-qā'imah***
And for their sakes O Powerful One, and by means of the obligatory prayers,

(11) اُلطُف بِنَا وَالمُسلِمِين   مِنْ كُلِّ عَينٍ لَآمَة (3)

ulṭuf binā wa 'l-Muslimīn ***min kulli ʿaynin lāmah (3X)***
Have mercy upon us and upon the Muslim from every evil eye.

(12) وَمِنَ العِدَا وَمِنَ الرَّدَى   وَمِنَ المَصَائِبِ عَامَّةْ

Wa mina 'l-ʿidā wa mina 'r -radā ***wa mina 'l-maṣā'ibi ʿāmah***
And from enemies, from wickedness and from all affliction all together

(13) وَعَلَيهِمُ يَا رَبَّنَا   مِنكَ الصَّلَاةُ الدَّائِمَة

Wa ʿalayhimu yā rabbanā ***minka aṣ-ṣalātu ad-dā'imah***
And send upon them my Lord, from You never-ending blessings

(14) ثُمَّ الصَّلَاةُ عَلَى الَّذِي   خَصَّصتَهُ بِمُكَالَمَة

Thumma 'ṣ-ṣalātu ʿalā 'l-ladhī ***khaṣaṣtahu bi-mukālamah***
And send blessing upon the one whom you distinguished by speaking to him (Muhammad ﷺ)

(15) يَاللّه بِهَا يَاللّه بِهَا   يَاللّه بِحُسنِ الخَاتِمَة

Yā Allāh biha, Yā Allāh biha Yā Allāh bi-ḥusni 'l-khātimah
O Allāh grant us, O Allāh grant us, O Allāh grant us a good ending

اللهُمَّ صَلِّ وَسَلِّمْ وَبَارِكْ عَلَيْهِ وَعلَىْ آلِه

Allāhuma ṣalli wa sallim wa bārik ʿalayhi wa ʿalā ʿālih

30 - Nahran min Laban

إنَّ فِي الْجنَّةِ نَهْرًا مِنْ لَبَنْ   لِعَلِيٍّ وَحُسَينٍ وَحَسَنْ لِعَلِيٍّ وَحُسَينٍ وَحَسَنْ

إنَّ فِي الْجنَّةِ نَهْرًا مِنْ لَبَنْ   لِعَلِيٍّ وَحُسَينٍ وَحَسَنْ لِعَلِيٍّ وَحُسَينٍ وَحَسَنْ

Inna fi 'l-jannati nahran min laban   li-'Alīyyin wa-Ḥusaynin wa-Ḥasan
Inna fi 'l-jannati nahran min laban   li-'Alīyyin wa-Ḥusaynin wa-Ḥasan

In heaven there is a river of milk, for 'Alī and Ḥusayn and Ḥasan
In heaven there is a river of milk, for 'Alī and Ḥusayn and Ḥasan

(1) يَا رَسُولاً قَدْ حَبَانَا حُبُّهُ فَضْلاً وَمَنْ   جُدْ عَلَينَا بِالتَّجَلِّيْ نَرتَجِي مِنكَ المِنَنْ

Yā rasūlan qad ḥabāna ḥubbuhu faḍlan wa man
Jud 'alaynā bi 't-tajalli nartajī minka 'l-minan

O Messenger whose love has rewarded us with favors and grants
Be generous to us with your manifestation, we seek from you all favors

(2) جِئتُ شَوقًا وَغرَامًا فِي هَوَى قَلبِي حَسَنْ   رَاجِيًا مِنهُ اِبتِسَاماً مَنْ لَهُ رُوحِي ثَمَنْ

ji'tu shawqan wa gharāman fī hawā qalbī ḥasan
rājiyan minhu 'btisāman man lahu rūḥī thaman

I came full of love and yearning and my heart full with desire
Hoping a smile from he for whom my soul is the price

(3) مِنْ فُؤادِي وَحَنِينِي وَحَنِينْ قَلبِي وَعَن   وَرأى الطَيرُ حَنِينِي فَبَكَى عَطفًا وَعَنْ

min fu'ādi wa-ḥanīnī wa-ḥanīn qalbī wa 'an
wa ra'ā aṭ-ṭayru ḥanīnī tabkī 'aṭfan wa 'an

From my heart, my yearning, the yearning of my heart and its moaning
The birds saw my yearning and started crying in sympathy

(4) وَصَلاَتِي وَسَلامِي لِلنَبِيِّ المُؤتَمَنْ   رَاجِياً حُسنَ الخِتَامِ بِالحُسَينِ وَالحَسَنْ

Wa 'ṣ-ṣalāti wa salāmi li 'n-Nabīyyi 'l-mu'taman
rājīyan ḥusna 'l-khitāmi bi 'l-Ḥusayni wa 'l-Ḥasan

My praising and blessings upon the trusted Prophet
Hoping to have a good end by means of al-Ḥusayn and al-Ḥasan

31 - ʿAla ʾl-Madīnah

عَلَى المَدِينَةْ عَلَى المَدِينَةْ   رَبٌّ بَلِّغْنَا زَيَارَة نَبِينَا
عَلَى المَدِينَة عَلَى المَدِينَة   رَبٌّ بَلِّغْنَا زَيَارَةْ نَبِينَا

ʿalā ʾl-madīnah ʿalā ʾl-madīnah rabbī ballighnā zayarat nabīynā
alā ʾl-madīnah ʿalā ʾl-madīnah rabbī ballighnā zayarat nabīynā
To Medina, onwards to Medina, my Lord grant us a visit to our Prophet
To Medina, onwards to Medina, my Lord grant us a visit to our Prophet

رَبِّ بَلِّغْنَا نَزُورْ الحَضْرَةْ   وَنشَاهِدْ احْمَدْ وَالقُبَّةْ الخَضْرَا
نِهْتِف جَمِيعاً يَا أَبَا الزَّهرَةْ   نحنُ زُوَّارَكْ فَكُنْ ضَمِينَا

Rabbī ballighna nazura ʾl-ḥaḍrah w iʾnshāhid Aḥmad wa ʾl-qubbaʾl-khaḍra
Nihtif jamīʿan yā abā ʾz-Zahrah naḥnu zuwwārak fakun ḍamīnā
My Lord grant us to visit his presence, to witness Āḥmad and the Green Dome.
So we all cry out: "O Father of Zahra, we are your guests, so give us your Guarantee!"

رَبِّ بَلِّغْنَا زِيَارَةْ طَهَ   وِنْشُوف الرَّوضَةْ وِنْصَلِّي حَدَاهَا
ونقُولْ يَا نَبِي يَا عَظِيمَ الجَاهْ   كُنْ لِيْ مُجِيراً كُنْ لِيْ مُعِيناً

Rabbi ballighna ziyarat Ṭāhā w ʾanshūfi ʾr-rawḍa w ʾanṣalli ḥdāha
Wi nqūl yā nabī yā ʿaẓīma ʾl-jāh kun lī mujīran kun lī mu ʿīnā
My Lord grant us to visit Ṭāhā, to see Paradise's Garden and pray in it
And to say, "O Prophet of high esteem, be my neighbor, be my aid!"

قَصْدِي اِلَى نَحوكُمْ أَسِيرُ   وَالْدمعُ مِنْ مُقلَتِي غَزِيرُ
وَالقَلبُ فِي حُبِّكُمْ أَسِيرُ   يَا قَلْبِي اِفرَح هَذَا نَبِينَا

Qaṣdī ilā naḥwikum asīru wa ʾd-damʿu min muqlatī ghazīru
Wa ʾl-qalbu fī ḥubbikum asīru yā qalbī ʾifrāḥ hādhā nabīyna
My firm intention and my steps are but to reach you, while from my eyes flow tears without cessation.
And my heart is a hostage to your love, while my heart rejoices, "there's our Prophet!"

سَاقِي الحُمَيَّا عَرِّجْ عَلَيَّ   وَاْسْقِنِي هَيَّا كَأساً وَفِياً
وَاْمدَحْ مُحَمَّدْ خَيرَ اْلبَرِيَّةْ   فَهُوَ اْلشَفِيعُ لِلْمُذنِبِينَ

Sāqī 'il-ḥumayyah 'arrij 'alayya ***wa 'sqinī hayyā ka'san wafīyya***
Wa'mdaḥ Muḥammad khayra 'l-bariyya ***fa-huwa 'sh-shafī'u li 'l-mudhnibīna***
Cupbearer of the attendees, tend to me, and pour me a full cup to drink
Praise Muhammad the best of creation, he is the intercessor of all sinners

اللهُمَّ صَلِّ وَسَلِّمْ وَبَارِكْ عَلَيْهِ وَعلَىْ آلِه
Allāhuma ṣalli wa sallim wa bārik 'alayhi wa 'alā 'ālih

32 - Āghithnā ya Rasūla-lLāh

الله الله أغِثْنَا يَا رَسُولَ الله

يَا عَظِيمَ الْجَاهْ عَلَيكَ صَلَوَاتُ الله

Allāh Allāh 'Aghithnā ya Rasūla-lLāh
Ya 'A◻īma 'ljāh 'alaika ṣalawātu-lLāh
Oh Allah oh Allah save us thruough the messenger of Allah
Oh prophet of great esteem, Allah's blessings upon you

عَبْدٌ بِالبَابْ يَرْتَجِي لَثْمَ الْأَعْتَاب   جُدْ بِالْجَواب مَرحَبًا قَدْ قَبِلْنَاه

'Abdun bi 'l-bāb yartajī lathma 'l'a'tāb Jud bi 'l-jawāb marḥaban qad qabilnāh

A slave waits at your door hoping to kiss your door steps, be generous with your reply, we welcome and accept it

أنتَ الْمَعْرُوفُ بِالْجُودِ مُقْرِي الضُّيُوف   إِنِّيْ مَلْهُوف أغِثْنِي بِحَقِّ الله

Anta 'l-ma'rūf bi 'l-jūdi muqri 'ḍ-ḍuyūf   inī malhūf 'aghithnī bi-ḥaqqi 'l-Lāh

You are well know for being generous and for honoring your guests; I am desperate, help me for the sake of Allah

أنتَ الْحَبِيبُ الأعْظَم سِرُّ الْمُجِيب   حَاشَا يَخِيب مَنْ لاذَ بِرَسُول الله

Anta 'lḥabību 'l-ā'ẓam sirru 'l-mujīb   ḥāshā yakhīb man lādha bi rasūli-lLāh

You are the greatest beloved one (to Allah) and the secret of the one who answers; he will never loose the one who takes refuge with the messenger of Allah

دَاوِ قَلْبِي وَامْنَحهُ سِرَّ الْقُربِ   وَاجْلِ كَرْبِي وَالحِقْنِي بِأهْلِ الله

Dāwi qalbi wa'mnaḥ-hu sirra 'l-qurbi   wa'jli karbī wa 'l-ḥiqnī bi āhli-lLāh

Treat my heart and grant it the secret of closeness to you; and remove my affliction and grant me to be with the people of Allah

صَاحِبَ ٱلْحَضرَةِ اَكْرِمْنَا مِنكَ بِنَظْرَةِ   يَا اَبَا الْزَّهْرَا وَالقَاسِمِ وَعَبدِ اللهِ

Ṣaḥiba 'l-ḥaḍrā 'krimna minka binaẓrā   ya abā 'z-Zahrā wa 'l-Qāsim wa 'Abdil-Lāh

Owner of the divine presence honor us by looking once at us; oh Father of Az-zahra and Al-Qasim and Abdillah

أنتَ الْحَبِيبُ بِذِكْرِك قَلْبِي يَطِيبْ   حَاشَا يَخِيبْ مَنْ لاذَ بِرَسُولِ اللهِ

Anta 'l-ḥabīb bi-dhikrik qalbī yaṭīb   ḥāshā yakhīb man lādhā bi rasūli'Lāh

You are the beloved one, my heart is healed with your remmemberance; **he will never loose the one who takes refuge with the Messenger of Allah**

انتَ الْمُختَارُ بِمَدحِكَ تُجْلَى الْأقْدَارْ   اجِرْنَا مِنَ النَّار بِجَاهِكَ يَا رَسُولَ اللهِ

Anta 'lmukhtār bi-madḥik tujla 'l-qdār   'jirna min 'n-nār bi-jāhik ya rasūla-lLāh

You are the chosen one, through your praise destinies become clear; save us from the fire for your sake oh Messenger of Allah.

33 - Ya Sayyidī ya Rasūla'Lah

يَا سَيِّدِي يَا رَسُولَ الله يَا مَنْ لَهُ الْجَاهُ عِندَ الله

إنَّ الْمُسِيئِينَ قَدْ جَاؤُوكَ بِالذَّنبِ يَسْتَغْفِرُونَ الله

Ya sayyidī ya Rasūla-lLāh Yā man lahu 'l-jāhu 'inda'l-Lāh
Inna 'l-musī'īna qad jā'ūk bi 'dh-dhanbi yāstaghfirūna Allāh

Oh my master o Messenger of Allah, you are the one whose rank is high with Allah; the sinners have come to you with their sins seeking Allah's forgiveness

يَا سَيِّدَ الرُّسْلِ يَا طَاهِرْ يَا غَايَةَ الْقَصْدِ وَالشَّان

صَلَّى عَلَيكَ العَالِي الْقَادِرْ فِي كُلِّ وَقْتٍ وَأَحْيَان

Yā sayyidā 'r-Rusli yā ṭāhir yā ghāyata 'lqadi wash-sha'ni
Ṣalla 'alayka 'l'āli 'lqādir fi kulli waqtin wa'aḥyāni

Oh master of the Messengers, oh pure one; you are the highest goal and aim; Allah the High the Powerul has blessed you in every moment and time

يَا سَيِّدَ الرُّسْلِ يَا طَاهِرْ عَبدُك عَلى بَابِكُم حَانِي

دَائِمْ لِمَعْرُوفِكُمْ شَاكِرْ فِي كُلِّ وَقْتٍ وَأَحْيَان

Yā sayyidā 'r-Rusli yā ṭāhir 'abduk 'alā bābikum ḥāni
Dā'im limā'rūfikum shākir fī kulli waqtin w 'aḥyāni

Oh master of the Messengers oh pure one, your slave is waiting with humility at your door; ever thankful for your favors, in every moment and time

34 - The Muḥammadan Qaṣīdah

سلام عَلَيْك يَا نَبِّيْ سَلامْ عَلَيْك سَيِّدِي

يَا نَبِّيْ يَا اِمَامَ الْحَرَمَين

Salām ʿalayk yā Nabī salam ʿalayk sayyidī

Ya Nabī yā Imama ʾlḥaramain

Peace upon you oh Prophet, peace upon you my master; oh prophet, oh leader of the two sanctuaries

مُحَمَّدٌ أشْرَفُ الأعْرَابِ وَالْعَجَمِ

مُحَمَّدٌ خَيْـــــرُ مَنْ يَمْشِي عَلَى قَــــدَمِ

Muḥammadun ashrafu ʾl-āʿrābi waʾl-ʿajami Muḥammadun khairu man yamshi ʿalā qadami

Muḥammad is the most honored one amongst Arabs and non Arabs; Muḥammad is the best one who ever walked on two feet

مُحَمَّدٌ بَاسِطُ الْمَعْرُوفِ جَامِعُهُ

مُحَمَّدٌ صَاحِبُ الإحْسَـانِ وَالْكَـــرَمِ

Muḥammadun bāsiṭu ʾl-maʿrūf jāmiʿuhū Muḥammadun ṣāḥibu ʾl-iḥsān wa ʾl-karami

Muḥammad is the one who spreads goodness and gathers it within him; Muḥammad is the owner of excellence and generosity

مُحَمَّدٌ تَاجُ رُسُلِ اللهِ قَاطِبَـــةً

مُحَمَّدٌ صَــــــادِقُ الأَقْوَالِ وَالكَلِـــم

Muḥammadun tāju rusli 'Llāhi qaṭibatan Muḥammadun ṣādiqu 'l-qawli wa 'l-kalimi

Muḥammad is the crown jewel of all the messengers of Allah; Muḥammad speaks the truth and his words are true

مُحَمَّدٌ ثَابِتُ الْمِيثَاقِ حَافِظُــهُ

مُحَمَّدٌ طَيِّـــبُ الأَخْـــلاقِ وَالْشِّيَـــمِ

Muḥammadun thābithu 'l-mīthāqi ḥāfiẓuhu Muḥammadun ṭayyibu 'l'akhlaqi wa 'sh-shiyami

When Muḥammad promises he true; Muḥammad possesses the most excellent of manners and traits

مُحَمَّدٌ رُوِيَت بِالْنُّورِ طِينَتُـــــهُ

مُحَمَّدٌ لَمْ يَــــزَلْ نُــــوْراً مِنَ القِدَمِ

Muḥammadun ruwīyat bin-nūri ṭīnatuhu Muḥammadun lam yazal nūran mina 'l-qidami

Muḥammad's constitution was nurtured with light; Muḥammad remains a light since pre-eternity

مُحَمَّدٌ حَاكِمٌ بِالعَدْلِ ذُو شَرَفٍ

مُحَمَّدٌ مَعْــــدِنُ الْأَنْعَامِ وَالحِكَـــــمِ

Muḥammadun ḥākimun bi 'l-ʿadli dhu sharafin Muḥammadun maʿdinu al-inʿāmi wa 'l-ḥikami

Muḥammad rules with justice and honor; Muḥammad is the substance of favors and wisdom

مُحَمَّدٌ خَيرُ خَلْقِ اللهِ مِنْ مُضَـــــر

مُحَمَّدٌ خَيْــرُ رُسْـــــلِ اللهِ كُلِّهِـــــمِ

Muḥammadun khairu khalqi 'Llahi min muḍarin Muḥammadun khairu rusli 'Llahi kullihimi

Muḥammad is the best of all creation, he hails from Muḍar; Muḥammad is the best of all Messengers

مُحَمَّدٌ دِينُهُ حَــقٌّ نَدِيــنُ بِـــهِ

مُحَمَّدٌ مُجْمَـــلاً حَقّاً عَلَى عَلَـــمِ

Muḥammadun dīnuhu ḥaqqun nadīnu bihi Muḥammadun mujmallan ḥaqqan 'alā 'alami

Muḥammad's religion is a truth we follow; Muḥammad all together is truth

مُحَمَّدٌ ذِكْــرُهُ رُوْحٌ لِأنْفُسِنَـــــــا

مُحَمَّدٌ شُكْرُهُ فَـــرْضٌ عَلَى الأُمَـــمِ

Muḥammadun dhikruhu rūḥun li anfusinā Muḥammadun shukruhu farḍun 'alā 'l-umami

Muḥammad's mention is the quickening of our souls; gratitude to Muḥammad is obligatory on all nations

مُحَمَّدٌ زِيْنَةُ الْدُّنْيَا وَبْهجَتُهَـــــــــــا

مُحَمَّدٌ كَاشِـــــفُ الْغُمَّاتِ وَالظُلَم

Muḥammadun zīnatu 'd-dunyā wa bahjatuha Muḥammadun kāshifu 'l-ghummātu wa 'ẓ-ẓulami

Muḥammad is the ornament of this world and its happiness; Muḥammad is the remover of sadness and darkness

مُحَمَّدٌ سَيِّــــــدٌ طَابَتْ مَنَاقِبُــــهُ

مُحَمَّدٌ صَاغَهُ الرَّحْمَــــــنُ بِالنِّعَــــم

Muḥammadun sayyidun ṭābat manāqibuhu Muḥammadun ṣāghahu 'r-Raḥmānu bi 'n-niʿami

Muḥammad is a master whose history is great; Muḥammad was molded with favors by The Merciful

مُحَمَّدٌ صَفْــوَةُ الْبَارِي وَخِيرَتُــــهُ

مُحَمَّدٌ طَاهِــــــرٌ مِنْ سَائِرِ التُّهَــم

Muḥammadun ṣafwatu 'l-bāri wa khīratuhū Muḥammadun ṭāhirun min sā'iri 't-tuhami

Muḥammad is the pure chosen one of the Fashioner of all things and His best creation; Muḥammad is innocent and pure of all acusations

مُحَمَّدٌ ضَاحِــكٌ لِلضَّيْفِ مُكْرِمُــهُ

مُحَمَّدٌ جَـــارُهُ وَاللهِ لَمْ يُضَــمِ

Muḥammadun ḍāḥikun li 'ḍ-ḍaifi mukrimuhu Muḥammadun jāruhu wa 'l-Lāhi lam yuḍami

Muḥammad smiles at the guest and honors him; by Allah, his neighbor will never be wronged

مُحَمَّدٌ طَابَــــتِ الْدُنْيَــا بِبِعْثَتِـــهِ

مُحَمَّدٌ جَـــاءَ بِالآيَــاتِ وَالحِكَـــــم

Muḥammadun ṭābati 'd-dunyā bi bi'thatihi Muḥammadun jā'a bi 'l-āyāti wa 'l-ḥikami

with Muḥammad's message the world was filled with goodness; Muḥammad came with verses and wisdom.

مُحَمَّدٌ يَـــوْمُ بَعْثِ الْنَّـــاسِ شَافِعُنَـــا

مُحَمَّدٌ نُوْرُهُ الْهَـــادِيْ مِنَ الظُّلَـــم

Muḥammadun yawmu ba'thi 'n-nāsi shafi'unā Muḥammadun nūruhu 'l-hādi mina' ẓ-ẓulami

Muḥammad will be our intercessor on the day of resurrection; Muḥammad's light will guide people out of darkness.

مُحَمَّدٌ قَائِـــــــمٌ للهِ ذُوْ هِمَــــــمٍ

مُحَمَّدٌ خَاتِـــــمٌ لِلْرُّسْـــــلِ كُلِّهِـــم

Muḥammadun qā'imun li-Llāhi dhu himamin Muḥammadun khātimun li 'r-rusli kullihimi

Muḥammad worships Allah with great devotion and effort; Muḥammad is the seal of the Messengers.

35 - The Closing Praise

اللهُمَّ صَلِّ وَسَلِّمْ وَبَارِكْ عَلَيْهِ وَعلَىٰ آلِه

Allāhuma ṣalli wa sallim wa bārik ʿalayhi wa ʿalā ʿālih

(1) الحَمدُ للهِ رَبِّ العَالَمِينَ. اللهُمَّ صَلِّ وَسَلِّمْ وَبارِكْ عَلَيْهِ وَعلَىٰ آلِه وَصَحْبِهِ أَجْمَعِينَ. جَعَلَنَا اللهُ وَإِيَّاكُمْ مِمَّنْ يَستوجِبُ شَفَاعَتَهُ، وَيَرجُوْ مِنَ اللهِ رَحْمَتَهُ وَرَأْفَتَهُ

AlḥamdulilLāhi Rabbi ʾl-ʿālamīn. Allāhuma ṣallī wa sallim wa bārik ʿalayhi wa ʿalā ʿālih wa ṣaḥbihi ajmaʿīn. Jaʿalana ʾl-Lāhu wa iyyākum mimman yastawjibū shafāʿatah wa yarjū mina ʾl-Lāhi raḥmatahu wa raʾfatah

All praise and thanks belong to Allāh, Lord of all the Worlds. O Lord, bestow Your blessings and grant peace upon our Leader Muḥammad ﷺ his family and all his companions. O Lord, make us and all present amongst those who receive his intercession, and hope for Allāh's mercy and favor.

(2) اللَّهُمَّ بِحُرمَةِ هَذَا النَبيِّ الكَرِيمْ، وَآلِهِ وَأَصحَابِهِ التَابِعِينَ عَلَى مَنْهَجَهُ القَوِيمْ، اجعَلنَا مِنْ خِيَارِ أُمَّتِهْ، وَاسْتُرنَا بِذَيلِ حُرمَتِهْ، وَاحشُرنَا غَداً فِي زُمرَتِهْ، وَاستَعمِلْ أَلسِنَتَنَا فِي مَدحِهِ وَنُصرَتِهِ، وَأحيِنَا مُتَمَسِّكِينَ بِسُنَّتِهْ وَطَاعَتِهْ، وَأَمِتنَا اللَّهُمَّ عَلَى حُبِّهِ وَجَمَاعَتِهْ

Allāhumma bi-ḥurmati hadha ʾn-nabyyi ʾl-karīm wa ʿālihi wa asḥābihi at-tābiʿīn ʿalā manhajahu ʾl-qawīm, ijʿalnā min khiyāri ūmmatih, wa ʾs-turnā bidhayli ḥurmatih, wa ʾḥshurnā ghadan fī zumratih, wa ʾstʿamil alsinatanā fī madḥihi wa nuṣratih, wa aḥyina mutamasikīna bi sunnatih wa ṭāʿatih wa amitnā ʾl-Lāhumma ʿalā ḥubbihi wa jamāʿatih

O Allāh, for the sake of this great leader, his family and companions who followed his paht, make us amongst the best of his Community, cover us with his sanctity. Gather us tomorrow in his group. Use our tongue in praising and defending him. Make us to live holding firmly to his Path (sunnah) and obey him, and make us die loving him and his Community.

(3) اللَّهُمَّ ادخِلنَا مَعَهُ الجَنَّةَ فَإِنَّهُ أَوَّلُ مَنْ يَدخُلُهَا، وَأَنْزِلنَا مَعَهُ فِي قُصُورِهَا فَإِنَّهُ أَوَّلُ
مَنْ يَنزِلُهَا، وَأَرْحَمنَا يَومَ يَشفَعُ لِلخَلاَئِقِ فَتَرحَمُهَا

*Allāhumma adkhilna maʿahu 'l-jannata fa-innahu awwalu man yadkhuluhā,
wa anzilnā maʿahu fī quṣūrihā fa innahu awwalu man yanziluhā, wa 'r-ḥamnā
yawma yashfaʿu li 'l-khalā-iqi fa-tarḥamuhā*

O Lord, please cause us to enter the Garden with him, for indeed, he is the first to
enter it, and cause us to enter its castles together with him for verily he is the first
to enter them. Have compassion on us on the day he intercedes for all creation,
for You have mercy upon all of them,

(4) اللَّهُمَّ ارزُقنَا زِيَارَتَهُ فِي كُلِّ سَنَةٍ، وَلاَ تَجعَلنَا مِنَ الغَافِلِينَ عَنكَ وَلا عَنهُ قَدْرَ سِنَة

*Allāhumma 'rzuqnā ziyaratahu fī kulli sanah, wa lā tajʿalnā mina 'l-ghāfilīna
ʿanka wa lā ʿanhu qadra sinah*

O Lord, please give us the opportunity to visit him every year. Do not make us
amongst those who are negligent in remembering You and remembering him
even for a little while.

(5) اللَّهُمَّ لا تَجعَل فِي مَجلِسِنَا هَذَا أَحَدًا إلاَّ غَسَلتَ بِمَاءِ التَوبَةِ ذُنُوبَهُ، وَسَتَرتَ بِرِدَاءِ المَغفِرَةِ عُيوبَهْ

*Allāhumma lā tajʿal fī majlisinā hādhā aḥadan illā ghasalta bi-mā'i 't-tawbati
dhunūbah, wa satarta bi ridā'i 'l-maghfirati ʿuyūbah*

O Lord, please render anyone in this assembly who has a single misdeed,
cleansed with the water of repentance; and conceal his sins with the garment of
forgiveness.

(6) اللَّهُمَّ إنَّهُ كَانَ مَعَنَا فِي السَّنَةِ المَاضِيَةِ إخوَانٌ مَنَعَهُمْ القَضَاءُ عَنِ الوُصُول إِلَى مِثلِهَا،
فَلا تَحرِمهُمْ ثَوَابَ هَذِهِ اللَّيلَةِ وَفَضلَهَا ٭(رَحِمَهُمْ الله)٭

*Allāhumma innahu kāna maʿanā fī 's-sanati 'l-māḍīyati ikhwānun manaʿahum
al-qaḍā'u ʿani 'l-wuṣūli ila mithlihā, fa lā taḥrimhum ajra hadhihi 'l-laylati wa
faḍlahā (raḥimahumul-Lāh)*

O Lord, last year there were friends amongst us who passed away (have mercy
on them) and thus were unable to be present this year because of Your Decree, so
please do not prevent them from partaking of the blessings and rewards of this
moment and its importance.

(7) اللّٰهُمَّ اِرحَمنَا إِذَا صِرنَا مِنْ أَصحَابِ القُبُورْ ووَفِّقْنَا لعَمَلٍ صَالِحٍ يَبقَى سَنَاهُ عَلَى مَمَرِّ الدُهُورْ

Allāhumma 'rḥamna idhā ṣirnā min asḥābi 'l-qubūr, wa 'waffiqnā li ʿamalin ṣāliḥinn yabqā sanāhu ʿalā mamarri 'd-duhūr

O Lord, have compassion upon us when we become the dwellers of the grave, and provide us with the earnest attempt to do good deeds that will remain shining throughout time,

(8) اللّٰهُمَّ اجْعَلنَا لآلآئِكَ ذَاكِرِينْ، ولِنَعْمَائِكَ شَاكِرِينْ، وَلِيوم لِقَائِكَ مِنَ الذَاكِرِينْ، أَحْيِنَا بِطَاعَتِكَ مَشغُولِينْ، وَإِذَا تَوَفَّيتَنَا فَتَوَفَّنَا غَيرَ مَفتُونِينَ وَلا مَخذُولِينْ، وَاخْتُم لَنَا مِنكَ بِخَيرٍ أَجمَعِينْ

※(اللّٰهُمَّ اِكفِنَا شَرَّ الظَالِمِينْ — 3 مرات)※

Allāhumma 'jʿalna li-'ālā-'ika dhākirīn, wa linaʿmā'ika shākirīn, wa li-yawmi liqā'ika mina 'dh-dhākirīn, wa aḥyinā biṭāʿatika mashghūlīn, wa idhā tawaffaytanā fa-tawaffanā ghayra maftūnīnā wa lā makhdhūlīn, wakhtum lanā minka bi-khayrin ajmaʿīn (Allāhumma 'kfinā sharra 'ẓ-ẓālimīn- 3 times)

O Lord, please make us amongst those who appreciate and remember what You conferred upon us, and be thankful for Your favors, and recall the Day of Meeting with You. Make us live and be preoccupied with obedience to You. When You cause us to die, let it be without falling into temptation nor let us be forsaken. We beg You, conclude all our affairs with the best of endings. (Our Lord, ward from us the evil of oppressors, 3x)

(9) وَاجْعَلنَا مِنْ فِتنَةِ هَذِهِ الدُنيَا سَالِمِينْ

Wa 'jʿalnā min fitnati hādhihi 'd-dunyā sālimīn

Keep us safe from the temptations of this worldly life.

(10) اللّٰهُمَّ اِجعَلْ هَذَا النَبِيَّ الكَرِيمَ لَنَا شَفِيعًا، وَارزُقنَا بِهِ يَومَ القِيَامَةِ مَقَامًا رَفِيعًا

Allahumma 'jʿal hadhā 'n-nabīyya 'l-karīma lanā shafīʿā, wa 'rzuqnā bihi yawma 'l-qiyāmati maqāman rafīʿā

O Lord, makes this Noble Messenger our intercessor, and - because of his intercession bestow upon us a lofty position on the Day of Judgment.

(11) اللّهُمَّ اسْقِنَا مِنْ حَوضِ نَبِيِّكَ مُحَمَّدٍ صَلَّى اللهُ عَلَيهِ وَسَلَّمَ شَربَةً هَنِيئَةً مَرِيئَةً لاَ نَظمَأُ بَعدَهَا أَبَدًا ، وَاحشُرنَا تَحتَ لِوَائِهِ غَدًا

Allāhumma 'sqinā min ḥawḍi nabiyyika Muḥammadin ṣallalLahu ʿalayhī wa sallama sharbatan hanī'atan marī'atan lā naẓmā'ū baʿdahā abadan, wa 'ḥshurnā taḥta liwā'ihī ghadan

O Lord, let us quench our thirst from the Pond of our Prophet Muḥammad ﷺ with an easy and unhurried drink that will cause us to thirst nevermore and gather us under his Banner tomorrow.

(12) اللّهُمَّ اغفِرْ لَنَا بِهِ وَلآبَائِنَا وَلأُمَّهَاتِنَا، وَلِمَشَايخِنَا وَذَوِيْ الحُقُوقِ عَلَينَا، وَلِمَنْ أَجرَى هَذَا الخَيرَ فِي هَذِهِ اللَّيلَةْ، وَلِجَمِيعِ المُؤمِنِينَ وَالمُؤمِنَاتْ، وَالمُسلِمِينَ وَالمُسلِمَاتْ، الأَحيَاءِ مِنهُمْ وَالأَموَاتْ

Allāhumma 'ghfir lanā bihi wa li-'ābā'inā wa li-ummahātinā, wa li-mashāyikhinā wa dhawi 'l-ḥuqūqi ʿalayna, wa li-man ajra hadhā 'l-khayr fī hadhihi 'l-laylah, wa li-jamiʿi 'l-mu'minīna wa 'l-mu'mināt, wa 'l-muslimīna wa 'l-muslimāt, al'ḥyā'i minhum wa 'l-amwāt

O Lord, for the sake of his high esteem with You, forgive us, our fathers, our mothers, our teachers, and those to whom we are obliged, as well as those who organized this honored assembly on this night, all believers men and women and all Muslims, men and women, the living as well as those who have passed on.

(13) إِنَّكَ قَرِيبٌ مُجِيبُ الدَّعَوَاتْ *(**وَقَاضِيَ الحَاجَاتْ**–3 مرات)* وَغَافِرِ الذُّنُوبِ وَالخَطِيئَاتْ *(**يَا أَرحَمَ الرَّاحِمِينْ**– 3 مرات)*

Innaka qarībun mujību 'd-daʿawāt (wa qāḍiya 'l-ḥājāt- 3 times)
Wa ghāfiru 'dh-dhunūbi wa 'l-khaṭī'āṭ (yā arḥama 'r-rāḥimīn – 3 times)

Verily You are The Near, Answerer of all prayers, (and granting all needs), and forgiving all sins and misdeeds, (O Most Merciful of the Merciful.)

(14) وَصَلَّى اللهُ عَلَى سَيِّدِنَا مُحَمَّدٍ وَعَلى آلِهِ وَصَحبِهِ وَسَلَّمْ، سُبْحَانَ رَبِّكَ رَبِّ العِزَّةِ عَمَّا يَصِفُونْ وَسَلامٌ عَلَى المُرسَلِينَ وَالحَمدُ للهِ رَبِّ العَالَمِينْ

Wa ṣallalLahu ʿalā sayidinā Muhammadin wa ʿalā 'ālihī wa ṣaḥbihī wa sallam. Subḥāna rabbika rabbi 'l-ʿizzati ʿammā yaṣifūn, wa salāmun ʿalā 'l-mursalīn wa 'lḥamdulilLāhi rabbi 'l-ʿālamīn

May Allāh's blessings be upon Muḥammad ﷺ his family and companions and grant them peace. Glory to thy Lord, the Lord of Honour and Power! (He is free) from what they ascribe (to Him)! And peace be upon the Messengers, and Praise be to the Lord of the worlds. Āmīn.

(الفاتحة)

Al-Fātiḥa

Original Songs by Ali al-Sayed

36- Words

I try to praise you ﷺ with words
But words only veil your greatness
What can one say to praise you?
Can glory be described?

I try to praise with words
But I usually get in the way
And if I is no longer there
Who would be praising who?

I try to praise you with words
As many before me have tried
Though their words are better than mine
They too must have felt ashamed

Everything has been said about you ﷺ
Everything which words could say
Yet my love compels me to praise you
Even if with the same words

The words which best describe you ﷺ
Are the words of your Creator
Each word He used to describe you ﷺ
Struck down all limits and restraints

"And you are of a tremendous character"
"And we have given you the fountain of abundance"
"And we will continue to give you until you are pleased..."
"Say if you love Allāh then follow me, Allāh will love you ..."
"Allāh and his angels continuously send blessings on the Prophet..."

37 - They Say, 'He's Just a Man'

They say, 'he's just a man like us,
Like us - he's just a man'
They say, 'he's just a man like us,
Like us - he's just a man'

Have they received revelation,
God's Uncreated Words?
And when they speak,
is their speech considered God's
Words?

They say, 'he's just a man like us,
Like us - he's just a man'
They say, 'he's just a man like us,
Like us - he's just a man'

Did they travel the Heavens
With their bodies in a blink?
Or drew nearer to their Lord
Than two bow's length?

They say, 'he's just a man like us,
Like us - he's just a man'
They say, 'he's just a man like us,
Like us - he's just a man'

Did the moon split in two
By the gesture of their hand?
And did water flow from their
palms
Enough for a thousand men?

They say, 'he's just a man like us
Like us - he's just a man'
They say, 'he's just a man like us
Like us - he's just a man'

Muḥammad ﷺ is a man
But not a man like us.
Muḥammad ﷺ is a diamond
And we are pebble rocks!

They say, 'he's just a man like us,
Like us - he's just a man'
They say, 'he's just a man like us,
Like us - he's just a man'

Muḥammad ﷺ is a man
But not like you and me!
If Muḥammad ﷺ never was
No other man would be!

They say, 'he's just a man like us,
Like us - he's just a man'
They say, 'he's just a man like us,
Like us - he's just a man'

38 - The Secret of Existence

The sun of guidance has risen
With the birth of Muḥammad ﷺ
And creation was given
The secret of existence (2)

Allāhumma ṣalli wa sallim ʿalā nūri ʾl-hudā
Allāhumma ṣalli wa sallim ʿalā badri ʾd-dujā (2)

He was created from His light
From the light of Allāh
And this light was dressed with more light
And then more and then more and then more (2)

Allāhumma ṣalli wa sallim ʿalā nūri ʾl-hudā
Allāhumma ṣalli wa sallim ʿalā badri ʾd-dujā (2)

When Allāh sent His mercy
To creation everywhere
He said the name of My Mercy
Is My beloved Muḥammad ﷺ (2)

Allāhumma ṣalli wa sallim ʿalā nūri ʾl-hudā
Allāhumma ṣalli wa sallim ʿalā badri ʾd-dujā (2)

Allāh said if you really love me
You must love Muḥammad ﷺ
For you don't really love me
If you don't love Muḥammad ﷺ (2)

Allāhumma ṣalli wa sallim ʿalā nūri ʾl-hudā
Allāhumma ṣalli wa sallim ʿalā badri ʾd-dujā (2)

39- My True Religion

The love of Muḥammad ﷺ and his family
Is my true religion, my reason to be
And if when I die my sins are too many
The love of Muḥammad ﷺ will rescue me
The love of Muḥammad ﷺ will rescue me (2)

Allāhumma ṣalli ʿalā ʾl-Muṣṭafā, Allāhumma ṣalli ʿalā ʾl-Muṣṭafā Ḥabībnā Muḥammad ʿalayhi ʾs-salām, Ḥabībnā Muḥammad ʿalayhi ʾs-salām, (2)

May God bless the Bedouin for the question he asked
Which unveiled the secret of the power of love
The answer to which made Abu Bakr dance
You'll be with the ones whom you love
You'll be with the ones whom you love (2)

Allāhumma ṣalli ʿalā ʾl-Muṣṭafā, Allāhumma ṣalli ʿalā ʾl-Muṣṭafā Ḥabībnā Muḥammad ʿalayhi ʾs-salām, Ḥabībnā Muḥammad ʿalayhi ʾs-salām, (2)

For Allāh to love you obey, his command
which says if you love me, then follow Muḥammad ﷺ
to follow Muḥammad ﷺ you must love Muḥammad ﷺ
For how can you follow that which you don't love?
For how can you follow that which you don't love? (2)

Allāhumma ṣalli ʿalā ʾl-Muṣṭafā, Allāhumma ṣalli ʿalā ʾl-Muṣṭafā Ḥabībnā Muḥammad ʿalayhi ʾs-salām, Ḥabībnā Muḥammad ʿalayhi ʾs-salām, (2)

If you love Muḥammad ﷺ you must love everyone
For his light is truly inside everyone
He's the mercy sent to every one
Only through love can we become one
Only through love can we become one

Allāhumma ṣalli ʿalā ʾl-Muṣṭafā, Allāhumma ṣalli ʿalā ʾl-Muṣṭafā Ḥabībnā Muḥammad ʿalayhi ʾs-salām, Ḥabībnā Muḥammad ʿalayhi ʾs-salām, (2)

40 - My Nation

"My nation, my nation"
His tears soaked the ground
He asked while prostrating
For hours on end
"My nation, my nation"
My lord forgive them
Grant them salvation
And a happy end (2)

Allāhumma ṣalli 'alā Muḥammad
Allāhumma ṣalli 'alāyhi wa sallim (2)

His nation His nation
Is everyone
In this creation
And in others as well
His nation his nation
Are you and me
All those before us
And those who will be (2)

Allāhumma ṣalli 'alā Muḥammad
Allāhumma ṣalli 'alāyhi wa sallim (2)

"My nation, my nation"
At his blessed birth
He made a prostration
And uttered those words
"My nation, my nation"
At his blessed death
My nation he whispered
With his last breath (2)

41 - Let Us Celebrate

Let us celebrate
The birth of Muḥammad ﷺ
Let us celebrate
Ṣall-Allāhu ʿalayh
Let us celebrate
The coming of mercy
Let us celebrate
Ṣall-Allāhu ʿalayh (2)

Let us be happy
Let us rejoice
Let us sing together
with one voice
Ṣall-Allāhu ʿalā sayyidinā
Muḥammad (2)

Let us join the moon
Let us join the stars
Let us sing his praise
Ṣall-Allāhu ʿalayh
Let us join the angels
Let us join the heavens
Let us sing his praise
Ṣall-Allāhu ʿalayh (2)

Let us be happy
Let us rejoice
Let us sing together with one voice
Ṣall-Allāhu ʿalā sayyidinā
Muḥammad (2)

Let us praise our Prophet
Let us sing his praise
Let us show our love
Ṣall-Allāhu ʿalayh
Let us praise with words
Let us praise with tears
Let us show our love
Ṣall-Allāhu ʿalayh (2)

Let us be happy
Let us rejoice
Let us sing together
with one voice
Ṣall-Allāhu ʿalā sayyidinā
Muḥammad (2)

If we praise our Prophet,
If we sing his praise
Allāh will bless us
Ṣall-Allāhu ʿalayh
Allāh loves those who love His
beloved
Allāh will bless us
Ṣall-Allāhu ʿalayh (2)

Let us be happy
Let us rejoice
Let us sing together
with one voice
Ṣall-Allāhu ʿalā sayyidinā
Muḥammad (2)

42 - Just One Look

Just one look is all I ask
From the one whose name is praise
The happiest one is the one upon
Whom shines your face

Ya rasūlallāh unẓar ḥālanā
ya ḥabīballāh ishfaʿ lanā

In your presence the stars disappear
The moon hides its face
For how can they bare to exist?
In the presence of such grace

Ya rasūlallāh unẓar ḥālanā
ya ḥabīballāh ishfaʿ lanā

The Angels of earths and heavens
Are enamored by your face
And the Lord of earths and heavens
Sends blessings on those who praise

Ya rasūlallāh unẓar ḥālanā
ya ḥabīballāh ishfaʿ lanā

If mercy was not your name
I would not have dared to ask
For how could a dirty beggar
Dare ask to see the king

Ya rasūlallāh unẓar ḥālanā
ya ḥabīballāh ishfaʿ lanā

Of all the titles you were given
'His servant' was dearest to you
The highest of all honors
Is servanthood to you

Ya rasūlallāh unẓar ḥālanā
ya ḥabīballāh ishfaʿ lanā

43 - How Can I Praise?

Allāhumā ṣalli wa sallim ʿalā sayyidinā wa mawlanā Muḥammadin
ʿAdad ma fī ʿilmillāhi ṣalātan dā'imatan bi-dawāmi mulki'l-Lāhi

How can I praise the one on whom Allāh bestowed
The crown of Honor and Majesty
The one who was granted by his Lord
The station of Praise and Glory

Allāhumā ṣalli wa sallim ʿalā sayyidinā wa mawlanā Muḥammadin
ʿAdad ma fī ʿilmillāhi ṣalātan dā'imatan bi-dawāmi mulki'l-Lāhi

The one for whose sake Allāh created
All that exists in this creation
The one who is the master of the world
The owner of the highest station

Allāhumā ṣalli wa sallim ʿalā sayyidinā wa mawlanā Muḥammadin
ʿAdad ma fī ʿilmillāhi ṣalātan dā'imatan bi-dawāmi mulki'l-Lāhi

No mind can understand your greatness
No words can describe your beauty
Imagination can not imagine
The secrets hidden in your reality

Allāhumā ṣalli wa sallim ʿalā sayyidinā wa mawlanā Muḥammadin
ʿAdad ma fī ʿilmillāhi ṣalātan dā'imatan bi-dawāmi mulki'l-Lāhi

We come to you with nothing to offer
Except this love and this repentance
For not praising you as we should
So please grant us your acceptance

Allāhumā ṣalli wa sallim ʿalā sayyidinā wa mawlanā Muḥammadin
ʿAdad ma fī ʿilmillāhi ṣalātan dā'imatan bi-dawāmi mulki'l-Lāhi

44 - Come to Mercy

Come to mercy
Mercy Ocean
Ocean of All the worlds
Mercy to All the worlds (2)

Muḥammad ṣall-Allāhu ʿalayh
Muḥammad ṣall-Allāhu ʿalayh
Muḥammad ṣall-Allāhu ʿalayhi wa sallam

Come to forgiveness
To the door of forgiveness
Bring all your burdens here
And watch them disappear (2)

Muḥammad ṣall-Allāhu ʿalayh
Muḥammad ṣall-Allāhu ʿalayh
Muḥammad ṣall-Allāhu ʿalayhi wa sallam

Come to goodness
To the guide to goodness
To the spring of beauty
To the spring of bliss (2)

Muḥammad ṣall-Allāhu ʿalayh
Muḥammad ṣall-Allāhu ʿalayh
Muḥammad ṣall-Allāhu ʿalayhi wa sallam

Come to Love
Sweetest love
One drop is enough
To melt the world away (2)

Muḥammad ṣall-Allāhu ʿalayh
Muḥammad ṣall-Allāhu ʿalayh
Muḥammad ṣall-Allāhu ʿalayhi wa sallam

45- We Love you Shaykh Nazim

Our Master, our teacher, our guiding light
Our love for you is great (Shaykh Nazim)
You saved us from the darkest night
Into the brightest day(Shaykh Nazim)

Our heaven is to be with you
no matter where you stay(Shaykh Nazim)
You are the sun in our lives
Please don't throw us away (Shaykh Nazim)

Thank you thank you for everything
You did for all of us (Shaykh Nazim)
How can we thank you, we don't know,
Our weakness we confess (Shaykh Nazim)

We love you, we love you, we love you so much
We love you, what else can we say? (Shaykh Nazim)
We love you, we love you, we love you so much,
We love you, what else can we say? (Shaykh Nazim)

May Allah give you long life
Health and happiness (Shaykh Nazim) x2

46 - Dedication

رَبَّنَا اغْفِرْ لِي وَلِوَالِدَيَّ وَلِلْمُؤْمِنِينَ يَوْمَ يَقُومُ الْحِسَابُ

Rabbana 'ghfir lī wa li-walidayya wa li 'l-muminīna yawma yaqūmu 'l-ḥisāb

14:41 "O our Lord! cover (us) with Thy Forgiveness - me, my parents, and (all) Believers, on the Day that the Reckoning will be established!

ISCA wishes to thank some of its constant ardent members for their unremitting support, and for their making the publication of this priceless jewel of a book possible. Some individuals who assisted asked us to dedicate the rewards of recitation from this book for the benefit of their loved ones. Others made this dedication secretly through their intentions, while yet others did not want us to mention their names. ISCA, its chairman, staff and members are grateful to each and every one of them.
Please dedicate your recitation to the souls of the people mentioned here and for the souls of the whole Nation of Sayyidina Muhammad ﷺ

The names of the donors and their loved ones:

Asif Dhar and family dedicated this book for the benefit of the souls of his mother Mumtaz binti Sara Banu.

Dr Tasneem Shamim and family dedicated this book to the loving memory of her grandparents Syed Abdul Ghani and Rahamathunissa Begum; and to her father Mohammed Munawarulla Turabi.

Muhammad Ijaz and Nasim Ijaz dedicate this book to the benefit of the souls of their parents.

Syed Shahzaman and Syed Mohsizaman dedicated this book to the benefit of:
Shah Sufi Golam Muqtader (R), Shah Sufi Hafez Bazlur Rahman(R), Shah Sufi Dr. Badiuz Zaman (R), Shah Sufi Syed Ali Ashraf (R), Kazi Amir Hossain, Shamsuddin Mia, Syed Afsar Ali, Shamsun Nesa, Abdur Rashid, Sakina Rashid, Syed Muniruzzaman, Shirin ZamanKazi, Syed Afzalul Haque, Sayyeda Nasim Ara, Syed Nasiruddin, Sakina Khatun, Kazi Syed Anwarul Haque, Najmun Nesa

Ali Foroughizadeh dedicated this book to Grand Shaykh Nazim Adil Al-Haqqani ق and his late wife Hajjah Amina ق.

Muhammad Adnan and family dedicate this book to the benefit of: Grandmother (Late) Sayyida Khatoon and parents Muhammad Iqbal / Shahnaz Begum and Shahid Usmani / Farhat Usmani.

Esha Sayed dedicate this book to the benefit of the soul of her mother Hashi Omair

Dr Wassim El-Harake dedicate this book to the benefit of the souls of: His mother Samya Yousuf Sleem and father Aḥmad Īlwan Alḥarakeh

Yasir, Asim and Amir Sheikh dedicate this book to: Bashir K. Shaikh and his wife A. Shaikh; Abdul Hamid Naik; and Abdul Ghani Mohammad.

Dr. Munir Sperling and family dedicate this book to the benefit of the soul of Hamza El Din who recently passed away.

Bahauddin and Karima Kylberg dedicate this book the souls of their grandparents, ancestors and their descendants and for the soul of their blessed spiritual mother Hajjah Amina Adil may Allah be pleased with her.

Dr Hisham Bazara and family dedicate this book to our beloved Prophet ﷺ and to his family, as-Sayyida Nafisa ؓ, Shah Baha'uddin Naqshband ق, Mawlana Shaykh Nazim ق, Mawlana Shaykh Hisham ق, and Mawlana Shaykh Adnan ق, and to our families and to the entire Ummah.

Shaykh Ahsan Sallman and family dedicate this book to his parents Muhammad Shafiq and Siddiqa Shafiq.

Nisar and Sara Sandhau dedicate this book to:
Nisar Ahmed Sandhu's family, those gone before and those still living.
Sara Sadhau 's Parents: Elmer Albert Mortensen, Jr.; and Margaret Eugenia Wright.
Paternal Grandparents: Elmer Albert Mortensen, Sr. and Dorothy Francis Reardon.
Maternal Grandparents: Eugene Stephen Wright and Helena Agnes Yeatman.
Paternal Great Grandparents: Jens L. Mortensen and Karen Peterson
Maternal Great Grandparents: James Harrison Wright and Flora Ann Amelia Wright.
Children: Steven W. Grylls, Jr; Maleekah D. Grylls; Ameenah L. Grylls; Jacqueline A. Dziedzic; Melissa L. Dziedzic; Rabiyah S. Ali (and Husband, Imran Ali).
Grandchildren: Elijah Camby; Emily Ray Foshee; Sage Lynette Dziedzic; Ahmed Nazim.
Brothers and sisters: Linda Helene Seybold; Christian Andrew Mortensen; Karla Woods; Haleema Nduwimana and to all my aunts and uncles, maternal and paternal, still living or deceased, and all my ancestors.

Nasreen Razak dedicate this book to her late father, Hamza Zaheed.

Zeeshan Ali and family dedicate this book to:
For the benefit of the blessed souls of Sultanul Awliya Shaykh Abdullah al-Faiz ad-Daghestani (q) and our beloved Saintly grandmother Hajjah Amina Adil (q), and for the holy presence of our Grandshaykh Sultanul Awliya Mawlana Shaykh Muhammad Nazim Adil al-Haqqani ar-Rabbani (q), the Light of our Lives our Shaykh Mawlana Shaykh Muhammad Hisham Kabbani al-

Haqqani ar-Rabbani (q), our Saintly mother Hajjah Naziha, and their blessed families, their followers and admirers.

Fatema Z. Akhtar and family dedicate this book to:
Abdul Hakeem (*marḥūm*); Khursheed Begum (*marḥūma*); Dr Waquar Ahmed (*marḥūm*); Hajji Abdul Qayyum; Najma Sultana Begum; And all our ancestors and our naqshbandi saints.

Marwa Azizi and Family dedicate this book to: Their parents and ancestors

Hisham Mandil dedicate this book to Mawlana Shaykh Hisham Kabbani

Notes

Lightning Source UK Ltd.
Milton Keynes UK
19 March 2011

169579UK00001B/6/A

9 781930 409439